KAMAKURA

鎌倉時代の彫刻

Published for the
Trustees of the British Museum by
British Museum Press

KAMAKURA

THE RENAISSANCE
OF JAPANESE SCULPTURE
1185-1333

鎌倉時代の彫刻

VICTOR HARRIS AND KEN MATSUSHIMA

Page 1 Detail of no. 35, Tateyama Shin

Pages 2–3 (from left to right)
No. 15, Mokkenren (Maudgalyāyana)
No. 9, Kichijō Ten (Mahāśri)
No. 22, Seitaka Dōji

Front cover Detail of no. 1, Kongō Rikishi (Agyō)

Back cover No. 28, Minamoto Yoritomo

© 1991 The Trustees of the British Museum

Published by British Museum Press
A division of British Museum Publications
46 Bloomsbury Street, London WC1B 3QQ

British Library Cataloguing in Publication Data
Harris, Victor
    Kamakura: the Renaissance of Japanese
    sculpture, 1185–1333.
    I. Title II. Matsushima, Ken
    III. British Museum
    732.72
    ISBN 0714114510

Designed by Harry Green

Set in Photina and printed in Great Britain by
BAS Printers Limited, Over Wallop, Hampshire

This exhibition has been organised by the British Museum, the Agency for Cultural Affairs, Tokyo, and The Japan Foundation, sponsored in the United Kingdom by Asahi Shimbun and Konica Corporation.

CONTENTS

MESSAGE

from
Tsuneaki
Kawamura,
Commissioner,
Agency for
Cultural Affairs,
Tokyo

I am delighted that this exhibition of Kamakura period sculpture is being held in the British Museum as one of the main events of the nationwide Japan Festival in celebration of the centenary of the Japan Society.

The period known as Kamakura dates from 1185, when Minamoto No Yoritomo defeated the Taira clan, until the decline of the succeeding Hōjō clan in 1333, a period of around 150 years. It is a period in which the newly flourishing military class came to the forefront of politics, replacing the old government by the aristocracy, and in which notable new cultural movements occurred reflecting the abrupt change in society. Sculpture of the age reflected the taste of the warrior class in a fashion for realism, and Buddhist images somehow became more human. For this reason the Kamakura period, in the history of Japanese sculpture spanning about 1,300 years until the nineteenth century, represents a renaissance of the art.

To enable a comprehensive appreciation of the subject a selection of forty exhibits, in total fifty-five pieces of sculpture including two National Treasures and twenty-eight Important Cultural Properties, has been made with due regard to historical changes, ranging from the powerful pieces of the early period to the skilfully contrived work of the late period, among them images made by the two great sculptors of the age, Unkei and Kaikei. I believe it is a significant point in world art history that Japan focused on realism in art in an age before the Renaissance occurred in Europe. Although international communication has improved in recent years, resulting in a higher level of cultural understanding, I believe that this exhibition is an especially meaningful opportunity to deepen an understanding of the old cultural traditions of Japan, and I trust that it will lead to closer relations between the peoples of the United Kingdom and Japan.

Finally, in addition to expressing my gratitude to those who have kindly allowed their sculpture to be exhibited, I should like to thank the Director of the British Museum and his staff for making the preparations for this exhibition, and all those people both in Japan and Britain who have contributed in some way. I pray for the success of the exhibition and through it for the enhancement of friendly relations between the peoples of the United Kingdom and Japan.

MESSAGE

from
Katori Yasue,
President,
The Japan
Foundation

The Kamakura period is the name given to the interval of 150 years from 1185, when Minamoto Yoritomo assumed control of the government of Japan. In contrast to the flowering of the aristocratic culture of the previous Heian period, this age represents the ripening of a down-to-earth realistic military culture. I am pleased that this exhibition, introduced as part of the Japan Festival held throughout the United Kingdom in commemoration of the centenary of the Japan Society in London, will enable everyone to catch a glimpse of the traditional art and culture of Japan.

The leading sculptors of the Kamakura period breathed their hearts and souls into their works, and this spirit remains in their sculptures even today, so that although cultures may differ the excitement of seeing the works transcends the centuries which have passed. Nowadays there is a tendency for the economic side of Japan to be emphasised, and it is sometimes rather an embarrassment for us still to be thought of as the inscrutable Japanese. But I firmly believe that the human expressions of sadness, anger and joy carved on the figures in this exhibition will illustrate the passions of the Japanese people and leave an emotional impression irrespective of culture, race or age.

Although geographically the United Kingdom and Japan are separated at the extremes of East and West, the development of transport and communication has encouraged us to feel closer. The movement around the world of both people and objects is increasing, and there is greater international accessibility to the media. However, on matters of cultural understanding we are sometimes at a loss for words. Our mutual ignorance can form a gulf between us like an ocean, threatening to become progressively deeper unless action is taken. The European Community is to be unified in 1992, and in addition to the lifting of barriers against the movement of material and people we can look forward to a broadening of cultural understanding. It is to be sincerely hoped that a similar path will be gradually widened between the United Kingdom and Japan.

Finally, I should like to thank those who have willingly offered to lend their valuable sculptures, and those British and Japanese who have been engaged for so long in the preparations for the exhibition. From the bottom of my heart I pray for the furtherance of mutual understanding between the United Kingdom and Japan through the success of this exhibition.

MESSAGE

from
D. M. Wilson
Director,
British
Museum

On behalf of the Trustees of the British Museum I should like to express my profound pleasure that this exhibition of Kamakura period sculpture from temples, Shintō shrines and museums in Japan is held in our new Japanese Gallery. The British Museum is rich in collections of artefacts from all cultures, and particularly rich in sculpture. We accordingly have a long tradition in the presentation of sculpture in our galleries, perhaps second to none in the world. The museum is therefore a most suitable place to be host to this most important event in the calendar of the Japan Festival and the greatest single loan ever outside Japan of Kamakura period sculpture.

In this day and age of growing understanding throughout the world such an exhibition is of considerable importance not only to demonstrate the richness of the Japanese cultural heritage, and the high level of the sculpture as an art form, but to bring to this country an easily assimilable approach to Buddhism, the living religion of Japan. Of all Buddhist arts Kamakura sculpture seems to be the most readily comprehensible – a bridge between the complex scriptures of Buddhism and its relevance to everyday life.

I am deeply grateful to The Japan Foundation and the Agency for Cultural Affairs, Tokyo, for organising the exhibition with us, and to the Asahi Shimbun and the Konica Corporation for their most generous support.

PREFACE

This exhibition presents the art of a significant epoch in Japanese history, the Kamakura period, when changes in society's views occurred similar to those of the Renaissance in Europe. In 1185 the Minamoto warrior clan wrested control of Japan from the aristocracy, forming a government at Kamakura several hundred miles from the capital of Kyoto, which was to last until 1333. Under this samurai government new temples were built, particularly in east Japan. Buddhism, which had been introduced to Japan in the sixth century from China and Korea, spread to become accessible to the rural population, and the Zen sect together with the artistic styles of the Song dynasty were introduced from China. Old models for the statues of Buddhist deities were revived as people searched for religious truths in the earliest teachings. Great temples, like the Kōfukuji and Tōdaiji of Nara that had been burnt to the ground during the wars, were restored, together with their eighth-century statuary, by a group of Nara sculptors who developed a style which was a mixture of the eighth-century fashions which had been strongly influenced by the Chinese T'ang dynasty, the so-called 'Tempyō' era style, and a new realism in the spirit of the warrior governors of society.

The wooden sculpture of the period was made hollow, from several blocks joined together to prevent splitting owing to changes in climate. It was realistically carved and coloured, and with the disturbingly lifelike inlaid crystal eyes unique to Japanese sculpture. Since virtually no comparable wood sculpture survives from medieval Europe, the warmth of the medium, compared with the stone of classic and medieval sculpture of the West, cannot fail but to bring a further dimension to the understanding of Western artists and scholars. Work of the several schools of the period, including masterpieces by Unkei, the 'Michelangelo of Japan', and Kaikei, his equally revered colleague, is shown here for the first time. The exhibits include, in addition to figures of Buddhist and Shintō deities, a number of realistic portrait sculptures of ascetics, priests and warriors, giving us a glimpse of the warmth and strength of character of some of the leading figures of Japan some seven centuries ago.

The opportunity to see such an array of the finest quality sculpture of the period is due to the generosity of The Japan Foundation, who also provided the photographs for this book, and in particular Kazuaki Kubo, Shoichi Toyoda, Futoshi Koga, Tomozo Yano and Sue Henny; the indefatigable efforts of the Agency for Cultural Affairs, Tokyo, in particular Akiyoshi Watanabe, Yasushi Nakamura, Kensuke Nedachi and Ken Matsushima who wrote the individual catalogue entries; the most necessary support of our friends of the Asahi Shimbun and the Konica

Corporation; and, of course, to the number of temples, shrines, museums and other bodies, listed below, who have so willingly lent their treasures for this occasion.

The editing and design of the catalogue have been done by Deborah Wakeling and Harry Green with their usual elegant creativity, and the exhibition has been designed by Geoff Pickup, Andrea Easey and Su Dale. Members of the Department of Japanese Antiquities have been, as usual, unfailingly supportive over an unusually busy period.

VICTOR HARRIS
Japanese Antiquities, British Museum

Lenders to the exhibition

Agency for Cultural Affairs, Tokyo

Amidaji, Shiga Prefecture

Amidaji, Yamaguchi Prefecture

Daihōonji, Kyoto

Daisenji, Osaka

Fukkōonji, Yamanashi Prefecture

Genkyūji, Yamaguchi Prefecture

Hōshakuji, Kyoto

Ishibaji, Shiga Prefecture

Jōrakuji, Shiga Prefecture

Jōshōan, Shiga Prefecture

Kaikōji, Kyoto

Kanazawa Bunko, Kanagawa Prefecture

Kōfukuji, Nara

Kongōin, Kyoto

Kōyasan Bunkazai Hozonkai and Kongōbuji, Wakayama Prefecture

Kōyasan Reihōkan, Wakayama Prefecture

Kōzanji, Kyoto

Kuwabara Ku, Shizuoka Prefecture

Manganji, Kanagawa Prefecture

Monjuin, Nara

Nakayamadera, Fukui Prefecture

Nara National Museum, Nara

Ninnaji, Kyoto

Seikōji, Chiba Prefecture

Shirayamahime Jinja shrine, Ishikawa Prefecture

Shōganji, Yamanashi Prefecture

Shōkōji, Ishikawa Prefecture

Shōmyōji, Kanagawa Prefecture

Takisanji, Aichi Prefecture

Tōdaiji, Nara

Tōgenji, Kyoto

Tokyo National Museum, Tokyo

Toyama Prefectural Government

Zendōin, Kyoto

Zenpukuji, Kanagawa Prefecture

INTRODUCTION

鎌倉時代の彫刻

Buddhism
and the
renaissance
of
Japanese
sculpture

A renaissance in Japanese religion and the arts occurred during the Kamakura period (1185–1333). The popularisation of certain Buddhist sects, and an introduction of new thinking both from within Japan and from abroad followed a violent reaction by the samurai warrior clans to some centuries of mismanagement by the aristocracy, resulting in a change to Japan's first military government, the Bakufu. Since Buddhism was propagated largely through the veneration of images of its various deities, the renaissance took a visible form in iconographic paintings and especially in the sculpture of the deities of the religion. The sculptures of this period are of a great variety, but they have in common an almost human presence which brings the ethereal concepts of Buddhism within the grasp of even those who have no knowledge nor interest in the subject.

Until 1185 Japan had been governed traditionally by a nobility ruled over by the Imperial line which had remained unbroken since the formation of the state some time during the first few centuries AD. Since the ninth century the nation had been virtually isolated from traditional ties with China and Korea, from where Buddhism had been introduced in the sixth century. The intervening three centuries saw the formation of an aristocratic society under the Fujiwara clan and the development of various pure Japanese art forms. There was a syllablic calligraphy used by women to write novels and poems; the arts of dyeing and embroidery of silken garments flourished; household and personal accoutrements were decorated in lacquer more refined than anything which had come from China in the past. But there was poverty in the rural areas in contrast to the luxurious life of the aristocracy, and the hold of the government weakened.

The Chinese system of central land ownership gradually broke down to give way to a growing feudalism. By the last decades of the twelfth century the great clans of samurai had controlling infuences both in the provinces and the capital, Kyoto. The Taira had usurped the influential position which the Fujiwara had enjoyed at the Emperor's court, yet their position was to prove unstable. Buddhist monasteries also had become powerful forces in their own right, rich holders of great estates, and with considerable garrisons of *sōhei*, or warrior monks, to protect their interests and enforce their views. Rivalry between the Taira and Minamoto clans culminated in war, in which the Minamoto eventually gained victory in 1185. Minamoto Yoritomo established the first Bakufu, or Curtain Government, in his military headquarters at Kamakura, several hundred miles from the Emperor's capital city of Kyoto.

The rise to power of the Minamoto had long-reaching effects on

Buddhism in Japan, for although the immense influence wielded by the great Buddhist temples over the Japanese nobility was curtailed, the leaders of the Minamoto and their allies, the Fujiwara, were enthusiastically religious and continued to build temples and sponsor the several sects of Buddhism. In Nara the Kōfukuji and Tōdaiji Temples were among those sympathetic to the Minamoto during the interclan wars. Both temples were assaulted and burned to the ground by the Taira, and their statuary dating back to the eighth century was lost. The images in the two temples were repaired chiefly by a group of Nara sculptors who have become known as the Kei school. During this period the artists of the Kei school produced masterpieces of wooden statuary which have never since in Japan been equalled in splendour and which provided models and inspiration for succeeding generations of sculptors. Under the sponsorship of the new samurai government they restored the figures in an adaptation of the original eighth-century Tempyō era style, which had evolved under the strong influence of T'ang China.

At this time relations with China were resumed after three centuries of relative isolation. Japanese monks again visited China as they had done in the Nara period and brought back with them philosophies and works of art which revived Buddhism in Japan. Paintings of Song dynasty China, in particular, revitalised the world of painting and sculpture. Among the religious teachings brought from China was Zen, which found immediate favour with the warrior class. Buddhism became more readily available to all levels of society through the evangelic activities of priests of the Pure Land sects. People searched for religious truths in the earliest teachings and revived old models for the images of Buddhist deities.

A new realism in the arts arose in the spirit of the warrior governors who now controlled society. The technique of making sculptures from several hollowed-out blocks joined together was developed to a high degree of skill and allowed a new naturalism which was dramatically enhanced by brilliant pigments and inset crystal eyes. In order to appreciate the sculpture it is essential first to consider the introduction and development of Buddhism in Japan, and the attitude of the Japanese craftsman to his subject and his materials.

Although anthropomorphic sculptures exist among the *haniwa*, low-fired red pottery figures which were set upright in the ground in the vicinity of the burial-mounds of the Kofun period (second to seventh centuries AD), and in the more distant past *dogu*, pottery dolls connected with agricultural and fertility rites, no other sculptural representations of the human figure are known which predate the arrival of Buddhism in Japan in the sixth century. All figural sculpture existing from between that time and the Kamakura period was religious, either Buddhist or Shintō, and kept in a temple or Shintō shrine. Portraits of human beings are mostly those of priests, and even those of secular figures like Minamoto Yoritomo (no. 28), the founder of the Kamakura Bakufu, was made for

Detail of no. 28

veneration and kept in a temple. An understanding of the sculpture can be achieved only by knowing something of both religions, for there is a complex relationship between Buddhism and Shintō (no. 36), and areas of overlap between the different sects in Japan. However, the development of Japanese sculpture is essentially through Buddhism, and the known sculptors of the Kamakura period were all affiliated to temple workshops.

Shintō

Shintō, the 'Way of the Gods (*Kami*)', was the state religion of Japan before the arrival of Buddhism from Korea during the sixth century AD. The *kami* are animistic gods, perceived in all aspects of nature. They exist in the nooks and crannies of houses, and inhabit streams, trees and mountains. There are *kami* sacred to all human work, including agriculture, warfare, and arts and crafts. The dead are all considered *kami* too. There are no readily definable moral precepts in the religion, yet the central rites of appeasement of the gods include acts of cleansing, gratitude, tolerance and obedience to tradition, which are central to the stabilisation of society. A creation myth recorded in the first Japanese written document, the *Nihon Shoki* (AD 720), describes a pantheon of great and minor beings, at the head of whom is Amaterasu Ō Mikami, the Sun Goddess, from whom the Emperors claim descent. Prior to Buddhism there was no custom of making images of the *kami* in human form, even though they had a homely relationship with the Japanese people. Extant wood and other sculpture from the Heian period most frequently represent the *kami* as true representations of male and female figures, often of aristocratic appearance, and sometimes even humorous (no. 37), in contrast to the frequently grotesque iconography of the Buddhist deities of the time.

Buddhism

Buddhism originated in India in the sixth century BC. Its founder was the Indian nobleman Siddhārtha Gautama, who rejected his luxurious upbringing to go out into the world and search for the solution to the ills and miseries of mankind. After years of ascetic practice, during which time he fasted so that his body withered and turned dark in colour, he finally attained spiritual enlightenment. Enlightenment (Japanese: *satori*) is the condition leading to becoming a Buddha. Siddhārtha is known as the historical Buddha, or Shaka (Japanese). Until the *nehan* (*pari nirvana*), or physical death of Shaka, he is said to have taught his doctrines throughout India. According to the teaching of Buddha the human experience is illusory. Suffering arises from the passions, which must be overcome in order to achieve true understanding. Salvation is through an understanding which transcends illusions of the world and a perception thereby of the true Buddha condition, which is the same for both men and women. Indeed, all living things can become Buddhas. The path to enlightenment is by a number of moral precepts which were either suggested by Shaka or developed by generations of followers, most of them bearing a strong family resemblance to those of other major religions. The enlightened condition is available to all the human race throughout all times in the past and time to come, and exists outside the limitations of all religious dogma and human knowledge. The original teaching did not involve the worship of images. Indeed, the enlightened Buddha is said to have become formless upon his death. His 'existence' was represented at first in India not by anthropomorphic images but by an unoccupied throne, or the Wheel of the Law, or by the Bodhi tree under which he was sitting when he achieved enlightenment.

On its progress eastward Buddhism travelled from India to China, and thence to Korea, first reaching Japan during the sixth century AD. It had changed over the centuries, incorporating ideas and deities from Jainism and Hinduism in India, and Confucian and Daoist philosophical concepts in China, as well as Shamanistic additions from those countries, South-East Asia and Korea. During the first few centuries of the Christian era the fundamentals of Buddhism broadened. The first sects, known as Hīnayāna (Minor Vehicle), were concerned with the progress of the individual towards enlightenment through his own adherence to the instruction of priests, who were assumed to be passing on the law of Buddha. Later, Mahāyāna (Greater Vehicle) Buddhism evolved in India, teaching that there is a plurality of Buddhas and other divine beings past, present and in the future. These divinities are directly approachable through worship, thus relieving mankind of much of the self-discipline and contemplation which the historic Buddha had to endure.

The scriptures of Mahāyāna Buddhism were translated from Sanskrit into Chinese, and from Chinese into Korean and Japanese, which had both borrowed and adapted the Chinese system of writing based on a vast vocabulary of characters. These influential documents include the *Hokekyō*, or Lotus *sutra*, which teaches the unique existence of an original Buddha. There are the Jōdo (Sukhāvatī), or Pure Land, *sutras*, which advocate a salvationist faith in Amida Buddha, the *Shōmankyō*, *Yuimakyō* and others. Very important during the Kamakura period was the *Hannyakyō*, which teaches an ultimate Ku, or 'Nothingness', as the essential enlightenment. In Japan Buddhism diversified further through the introduction of a number of different sects and an ever-growing population of deities, brought from the mainland mostly by Japanese monks who had travelled to Korea and China in search of knowledge. The esoteric sects known as Mikkyō (esoteric teachings) and the contemplative Zen stress the attainment of enlightenment during this life, either absolute or partial, through the means of various rituals or through contemplative practices. Others, like the several sects of Jōdo, the Pure Land, promised a salvation through faith in the merciful intervention of the Buddha Amida (Amitābha) and his emanations, such as the Bodhisattva Kannon. The faithful could hope for acceptance into Paradise upon death.

Although according to some teachings there is an infinity of Buddhas and universes, and the number of different recognisable deities is uncountable, the more frequently occurring Buddhist images can be grouped together in six simple classifications.

The Buddhas or Nyorai (Tathāgata)

These beings are the perfectly enlightened and include the historic Buddha, Shaka (Śākyamuni), and other Buddhas introduced by successive Mahāyāna sects. In painting and sculpture Buddhas are represented wearing the toga-like robes of monks, with either both shoulders covered or the left shoulder bare. A number of features usually identify them. First, their skin is golden, the colour which Shaka developed upon enlightenment. Their earlobes are long, a feature which they share with other divine Buddhist beings, and which according to one theory may derive from the custom of the ancient Indian aristocracy, of which Shaka was a member, of wearing heavy earrings. The head has a dome-shaped protuberance on the top, which indicates a superior intelligence. The hair is usually depicted in tight curls, which, like the toga, seems to have stemmed from Graeco-Roman influences, for there were Mediterranean sculptors active in Gandhara (now parts of Pakistan and Afghanistan), which is where this image derives, during the first few centuries AD. A more legendary explanation is that Shaka cut his long, wavy locks short upon resolving to go out into the world. A whorl of hair in the centre of the forehead, signifying the special wisdom of the enlightened, is called a *byakugō* (*urna*) and is often depicted by an inset precious stone or crystal. Three lines across the throat represent folds in the flesh. The fingers are slightly webbed, and the Wheel of the Law might be visible on the palms or soles of the feet.

SHAKA NYORAI   Forms of Shaka usually depict 'historic' episodes from the legends of his life. He is sometimes shown as a child with one hand pointing to the sky and the other to the earth in the attitude he took when as an infant he said that this was his last birth. Frequently in Japan he is shown in emaciated form, having descended from years of austere exercises in the mountains, at the point at which he achieved full enlightenment. Also very common, especially in paintings, is the *pari nirvana*, or death of Buddha, in which he is shown lying on his side surrounded by distressed disciples, various other living creatures and angelic beings. The most common form, however, has Shaka with his right hand raised palm outwards in a gesture of benediction (no. 18), and simply dressed in the classic garb of a Buddha, often accompanied by two Bodhisattvas, one on either side.

BIRUSHANA BUTSU, OR MAKABIRUSHANA (MAHĀVAIROCANA)
Roshana is the ultimate centre of esoteric Buddhism, the brightness of

whose wisdom exceeds that of the Sun, hence his appellation Dainichi, meaning literally 'The Great Sun'. All other Buddhas and Bodhisattvas emanate from Dainichi. The *Dainichi sūtra* and the *Kongōchō sūtra*, the two bases of esoteric Buddhism, describe the deities which derive from the power of Dainichi. There are two forms of Dainichi, both as Bodhisattvas. One representing the Kongōkai (Diamond World) holds his hands in the *chikenin* gesture with the hands in front of the breast and the index finger of the left hand pointing upwards and grasped by the right hand. The other represents the Taizōkai (Matrix World) and makes the *hōkaijōin* gesture, with the right hand resting on the left palm in turn resting on the lap, and with the thumbtips lightly touching.

YAKUSHI NYORAI (BHAIṢAJYAGURU)   He is also called Yakushi Ryuriko Nyorai (literally, 'medical teacher lapis lazuli light Nyorai'), who inhabits the lapis lazuli Jōdo (Pure Land Paradise). Yakushi was first introduced into Japan in AD 680 as the Buddha who bestows healing. He is usually flanked by Nikkō and Gakkō, the Bodhisattvas of sunlight and moonlight. A medicine jar is held in the left hand which is extended in the gesture of granting requests, and the right is held up with the palm facing outward. The Buddha has seven forms which, according to the *Yakushi sūtra*, should all be represented together. For convenience the seven are usually carved or painted in miniature on the halo of the main figure in the Tendai sect. This Nyorai is sometimes accompanied by the Jūni Shinshō, the Twelve Heavenly Generals who preserve the twelve vows of Yakushi, or as Yashajin (demonic gods) who protect the believer.

ASHUKU NYORAI   This Nyorai dispels anger, and in popular belief his name is found in the *Jōdo sūtra* together with that of Amida Nyorai. In esoteric Buddhism he is shown in the east of the Diamond World *mandala*, when his gesture is the *kongōin* – the right hand placed palm downward on the right knee with the finger pointing to the ground. He is often shown holding the hem of his garment with his left hand.

AMIDA NYORAI (AMITĀBHA)   Amida Nyorai presides over the Western Jōdo (Pure Land). Believers who call on his name will go to this Paradise, as a result of the forty-eight vows Amida made to save all beings. Amida occurs in three forms. As the Buddha of salvation for the Jōdo Shinshū sect he appears usually seated with his hands in one of the *seppōin* gestures (with the thumbtip touching one of the first three fingertips). Secondly, in both Jōdo and esoteric Buddhism he sits in meditation with his hands in the *jōin* gesture with the left hand held over the right palm upwards in the lap, and the thumbtips and one of the fingers on each hand touching. In the *raigō*, or welcoming attitude, Amida stands with the thumb and fingertip of the raised right hand touching, and the other hand held down and open. He is often flanked in this aspect by the two

Bodhisattvas Kannon and Seishi who are sometimes shown standing respectively with their hands clasped in prayer, and bearing a lotus upon which the believer is transported to Paradise upon death.

MIROKU (MAITREYA)   Miroku is the next Buddha to come, and is thus often represented in the form of a Bodhisattva, usually sitting with his right leg supported over the left knee, and with the fingers of his right hand meditatively touching his right cheek.

Bosatsu (Bodhisattvas)

The Bodhisattvas are beings who have reached the stage of enlightenment necessary for becoming a Nyorai but have elected to stay in the existence of phenomena in order to aid the enlightenment, or salvation, of all beings. They are usually clothed in princely garb, with the upper body bare, although draped with a *jōhaku*, or sash, and wearing a *mo*, a kind of long, pleated skirt, and richly bedecked with a crown and jewellery. Their hair is usually long, in contrast to that of the Nyorai, and is tied in bunches. Since they are the immediately accessible deities according to Mayāyāna Buddhism, they are often the principal deity in the main hall of a temple where the laity would be admitted.

FUGEN (SAMANTABHADRA) AND MONJU (MAÑJUŚRĪ)   These Bodhisattvas are said to have been brothers, princes alive at the time of Shaka. They are shown riding respectively an elephant and a lion, and accompany Shaka Nyorai. Fugen promotes the practice of Buddhism, and Monju represents the wisdom of Shaka.

KANNON (AVALOKITEŚVARA) AND SEISHI (MAHĀSTHĀMAPRĀPTA)
Together these Bodhisattvas accompany Amida Nyorai. Kannon is the prime Bodhisattva of all major sects, and as such has earned the popular title 'Goddess of Mercy', although the gender probably obtains from secular or extra-Buddhist interpretations. There are many forms of Kannon in esoteric Buddhism such as the eleven-headed (Ekādaśamukha, whose Bodhisattva head is surmounted by ten small Nyorai heads); the horse-headed Kannon; the thousand-armed Kannon (normally represented by a lesser number of arms symbolising the thousand); the Fukū Kenzaku Kannon (Amoghapāśa) who carries a noose with which to save all beings; and the Nyoirin Kannon (Cintāmaṇicakra) who relieves suffering by turning the Wheel of the Law (no. 17).

KOKUZŌ (ĀKĀSĀGARBHA OR GAGANAGAÑJA)   This Bodhisattva attends on Dainichi Nyorai and is essentially an esoteric figure. He represents the twofold virtue of wealth and wisdom and is the manifestation of Dainichi Nyorai in the Kongōkai (Diamond World), just as Jizō is the manifestation of the Buddha in the Taizōkai (Matrix World).

JIZŌ (KṢITIGARBHA) Jizō appears frequently alone in the guise of a shaven-headed priest. In his left hand he holds a *hōju* (treasure jewel) which is emblematic of the provision of wished-for virtue. In his right hand he carries a *shakujō*, or priest's staff, with a finial of loose iron rings which jangle and warn creatures, otherwise unaware, of his coming. He is engaged in the salvation of sentient beings throughout the present age of the world until the coming of Miroku as a Buddha. Jizō is especially concerned with the welfare of children, both living and dead, and as such is a very commonly found image in temples and roadside shrines. Jizō appears in the standard Bodhisattva form in the Taizōkai (Matrix World) *mandala* of esoteric Buddhism.

The Ten (Deva)

The Ten, or Heavenly Beings, derive mostly from the Brahmanic deities of ancient India, the earliest recorded of them being Bon Ten and Taishaku Ten (no. 4). The most frequently encountered grouping is the Shitennō, the Four Heavenly Guardians who protect the four directions against the enemies of Buddhism. They are Jikoku Ten, Zōchō Ten, Kōmoku Ten and Tamon Ten (no. 2). Dressed in armour or military tunics in T'ang Chinese style, some carry polearms, *vajra* (pronged implement of esoteric Buddhism) or other weapons. Their expressions are ferocious and they are shown in postures of violent movement. In addition there are the Kongō Rikishi (two strong deities of the Diamond World), otherwise called Ni-Ō (Two Guardian Kings, no. 1).

The Hachi Bushu, or Eight Companions, were gods outside Buddhism who were saved by Shaka and rehabilitated as his attendants. They guard the Buddhist law together with the Ten Disciples. Their names are recorded in the Lotus *sūtra* as Ten (Deva), Ryu (Nāga), Yasha (Yakṣa), Kendarupa (Gandharva), Ashura (Asura), Karura (Garura), Kinnara (Kiṃnara) and Magoraka (Mahoraga). Their pre-Buddhist Indian origin is shown by their body colouring and in their faces.

Larger groups of various Heavenly Beings are the Jūni Shinshō (Twelve Heavenly Generals, no. 6), the Jūni Ten (Twelve Heavenly Guardians) and many others. A number of individual Ten also occur. A favourite in Japan is Daikoku Ten (no. 37), a deity identified with the Shintō *kami* Ōkuninushi No Mikoto but deriving also from the Hindu pantheon. He has been revered in Buddhist temples since the development of the Ryōbu Shintō doctrine in the late Heian period, which claimed that the Buddhist and Shintō deities are aspects of the same beings. Daikoku is also one of the Seven Lucky Gods, who are not specifically Buddhist. Other Heavenly Beings include Jinja Taishō (no. 12), Kichijō Ten (no. 9), Benzai Ten, who is also one of the Seven Lucky Gods in popular belief, and Emma-Ō, Judge of Hell (see no. 19).

The Hachi Dai Dōji (Eight Great Youths) attend Fudō Myō-Ō. Their bodies are soft and childlike, and their expressions direct and emotional.

Human figures

Among the most important groupings are the Jūroku Rakkan (Sixteen Arhats) and the Jū Dai Deshi (Ten Great Disciples). These are both legendary followers of Shaka, whose images become more and more fantastic through the Kamakura period.

The Myō-Ō

The light of the Myō-Ō (Kings of Light) is the light of wisdom which emanates from Dainichi Nyorai, the central figure of esoteric Buddhism. Deriving originally from Indian deities, some of them have several arms or heads, and they have angry expressions although their dark blue bodies are in fact those of youths. They operate in the illusory world of human passions and emotions, evident from their expressions, although their purpose is to dispel such notions. Since their nature relates to human behaviour, they provide models for everyday use. Their power to save is through magical words (*mantra*). The Myō-Ō are found in groups of eight (Hachi Dai Myō-Ō) or five (Godai Myō-Ō). The most popular are Aizen Myō-Ō, Fudō Myō-Ō and Dai Gensui Myō-Ō. The most usual combination of five, the Godai Myō-Ō, are manifestations of the true natures of the five Nyorai of wisdom (Gochi Nyorai) of the Diamond World in their role as saviours. According to the *Shomuge sūtra*, they each have a prescribed iconography and are responsible for one of the five directions.

FUDŌ MYŌ-Ō (ACALA), OR 'THE UNMOVING', is a manifestation of Dainichi, occupying the centre. He has a single ferocious face and two arms in which he holds a weighted rope to ensnare wickedness and a sword to destroy it. Fudō is one of the most popular images in Japanese Buddhism of the Kamakura and later periods.

KŌZANZE MYŌ-Ō (TRAILOKYAVIJAYA) is a manifestation of Ashuku, occupying the East. He has three faces with three eyes and eight arms.

GUNDARI MYŌ-Ō (KUṆḌALI) occupies the South. He has one face with three eyes and eight arms.

DAIITOKU MYŌ-Ō (YAMANTAKA) occupies the West. He has six faces with three eyes, six arms and six legs, and rides a water buffalo.

KONGO YASHA MYŌ-Ō (VAJRAYAKṢA) occupies the North. He has three faces with five eyes and six arms. Kongō Yasha is sometimes known as Ususama in the Tendai sect.

AIZEN MYŌ-Ō (VIDYARĀJA), whose name signifies the passions, is unique among the Myō-O in having not a dark blue but a vermilion body. His head is surmounted by a *shishi* (lion-dog), and he is armed with several

Detail of no. 27

esoteric attributes, the *vajra* of five points, a *vajra*-handled bell, bow and arrows, and other implements. He sits on a vermilion lotus above a vase symbolising spiritual treasure (no. 21).

KUJAKU MYŌ-Ō (MAHĀMAYŪRI VIDYĀRĀJÑI) sits on a peacock. Venerated in Japan before the ninth-century popularisation of Mikkyō, this is the only Myō-Ō with a benign expression. Since the peacock will eat poisonous snakes, this deity will dispel all evils. He may have two, four or six arms.

Shintō and quasi-Shintō deities

Pure Shintō deities were often represented as aristocrats in court dress, as agricultural figures or even animals; or as a compromise between Buddhism and Shintō, in which case they were usually depicted as Bodhisattvas. For the most part wooden Shintō sculpture was made by different artisans from the *busshi* (guilds of specialist Buddhist sculptors) affiliated to Buddhist temples, and little is known of them. The work is often crude but can have a compelling beauty and always has a powerful presence.

Portraits

Portraits include those of the founders of sects, both historic and legendary, of the disciples of the historical Buddha, and of priests made either during their lifetime or just after their death.

Introduction of Buddhism into Japan

Something was no doubt known in Japan of Buddhism before its first recorded arrival during the Asuka period (AD 538–645), when the capital was situated at various places on the Asuka plain in the province known as Yamato (modern Nara Prefecture). According to the *Nihon Shoki* this occurred in AD 552, when an emissary from Paekche (Kudara – one of the nations of Korea) arrived at the court with a gilt-bronze figure of Shaka Nyorai, banners and *sūtras*, although the date 538 is considered to be more likely for this event. There had already been both military and peaceful contacts with the East Asian continent for some centuries. There were, for example, groups of emissaries of several hundred people dispatched to China every seven years for a period at the beginning of the fifth century. Immigrant metal craftsmen and lacquerers of Korean and Chinese descent had formed hereditary guilds in Japan. The makers of iron and gilt-bronze arms and horse-trappings known as *kuratsukuri* (saddle makers), active during the Kofun period, must have been aware of the existence of the gilt-bronze Buddhist images used in temples in China and Korea. Even so, the *Nihon Shoki* history of Japan (AD 720) tells of the Emperor Kimmei's delight and surprise upon hearing what Buddhism had to offer.

At the time Shintō was established as the state religion, with the Emperor enjoying political primacy backed up by the legend of his descent from the Sun Goddess Amaterasu, and hence a semi-divine and priestly status. The nation was governed through a network of Shintō shrines in which the gods were never depicted in human form but represented by an object, usually a sword, mirror or jewel signifying their physical manifestation. The concept of an image for worship and the idea of spiritual salvation must have been quite alien for the Emperor and his Shintōist ministers. But the existing system of government through a national religion provided a strong basis for the eventual propagation of Buddhism throughout Japan.

At first opinions were divided as to whether worship of the image from Korea should be allowed. The opinion of Iname, a minister from the Soga family, was that Japan should worship the Buddha since all the surrounding nations were doing so. A minister from the Mononobe family countered that it might anger the many gods of Japan who were used to being fêted, each with its own seasonal festivity. At first the Soga were allowed to worship the image in private, but when a plague occurred Buddhism was blamed, the Soga temple destroyed, and the image thrown into a canal at Naniwa (near present-day Osaka). This episode made a lasting impression, and many copies of a triad of Shaka and two Bodhisattvas said to have been rescued from the canal were made during the Kamakura period for the Jōdo sect, presumably in respect for their antiquity (no. 38). This type of rennaissance style is known as Zenkōji, after the name of the temple where the original rescued images are said to have been taken. The disagreement between the Soga and Mononobe became a desperate struggle at the end of which the Soga prevailed, and the way was clear for the spread of Buddhism.

In 593 the Shitennōji Temple was built at Naniwa by the Prince Regent Shōtoku Taishi, who later became canonised as the virtual founder of Buddhism in Japan, and whose images were to be revered in temples irrespective of sect. Many figures of Shōtoku Taishi were made in the Kamakura period (nos 23, 24). Shōtoku Taishi established also the Hōryūji Temple near Nara, which survives to this day, a tribute to the same skills and understanding of timber construction which later made possible the magnificent lasting statues of the Kamakura period. In the following year Buddhism was declared a national religion, to occupy the attentions of successive emperors and military rulers in parallel with the native Shintō.

Sculptural styles before the Kamakura renaissance

Buddhist sculpture before the establishment of the Kamakura Bakufu in 1185 was for the most part easily divisible into three major periodic groups. There was the Asuka style, when the capital was at Asuka, followed by the Nara style, from the period when the capital moved to nearby Nara, between AD 710 and 794, and the Heian style, from the period when the capital was at Heian (modern Kyoto) between the years 794 and 1185.

The moves of capital were not only the result of the Japanese tendency to change location following calamity, or the death of an emperor, but also a means of breaking the control exerted by the priesthood as temples and monasteries grew up in and around the seats of secular power.

Asuka period

The earliest Buddhist sects in Japan were Mahāyāna (Greater Vehicle), which was characterised by a proliferation of deities, but there were relatively few which were widely adopted. The most important were primarily the historical Buddha (Shaka), the Buddha yet to come (Maitreya), and a number of Bodhisattvas, chief among whom was Kannon (Avalokiteśvara). In addition there were relatively minor angelic Heavenly Beings and attendants.

Broadly speaking, the Asuka style followed the style of the Buddhist stone and bronze sculpture of China during the six dynasties period. However, Buddhism had originated in India, and the influence of Indian art had played a major role in the development of both iconography and style. The clothing, in particular, of the early sculpture is highly reminiscent of the images of Gandhara in the north-west of the Indian subcontinent. Among these characteristics are the loose robes draped over one or both shoulders, falling to well below the knees. In the Asuka period the robes were shown as rather heavy and fell in regular, stylised folds.

The method of dressing the hair of the Nyorai Buddhas in a mass of tight curls probably derives also from the late classical Mediterranean world. The arms, particularly of the Nyorai and Bodhisattvas, are long, the bodies slender and straight upright. The faces, hands and feet are disproportionately long and rectangular in general shape. The eyes are narrow, elongated, almond shapes, sometimes almost closed, and the mouths form the characteristic and enigmatic archaic smile.

Both wood and bronze were used to make images during this period. Bronze pieces were cast by the lost-wax process. In this method a core largely of clay and sometimes on a wooden frame was first built up in the rough shape of the desired figure. A layer of wax covered the core, and the form of the deity was sculpted in the wax. The whole was then covered with a further mould of clay, supported on the core by transverse metal rods. The wax was then melted out, leaving a cavity between the core and the mould into which the molten bronze could be poured. The core and mould were then broken away. Usually the figure was then gilded using an amalgam of gold in mercury, which was applied on to the heated bronze in much the same way as a plumber wipes a joint.

Guilds of immigrant continental craftsmen had existed since the Kofun period, and these craftsmen made the first Buddhist bronzes. The earliest dated bronzes extant in Japan are a Yakushi triad made in AD 607 and a Shaka triad made in AD 623 by Kura Tsukuri No Tori (Tori, the saddle maker), from one of the aforementioned guilds. By the eleventh century guilds of *busshi* were well-established, flourishing in Kyoto and Nara particularly during the Kamakura period.

Nara period (AD 710–94)

A sudden change came about in the early Nara period, when a new and bigger capital was built in Nara. The influence of Korea, until this time dominant, then waned, and Japan turned to China for its cultural inspiration. Buddhism continued to expand in Nara. In AD 741 the Emperor Shōmu (r. 724–49) ordered the construction of temples and nunneries in every province, known as the *kokubunji*. He started the building of an immense bronze figure of the Buddha Birushana in a temple at Nara, the Tōdaiji, which was completed in 752. The parallel between the Emperor's own position as a direct descendant of Amaterasu Ō Mikami, the Shintō sun deity, and the position of Dainichi Nyorai as the centre of the Buddhist cosmos may explain the fervour with which the project was carried out.

The sculpture of this period became altogether more sophisticated, with bodies of recognisably human proportions in place of the elongated, stylised earlier pieces. Images were made in the style of early T'ang dynasty China (seventh to eighth centuries), with fuller figures dressed in the graceful, flowing robes fashionable among the Chinese aristocracy. The eyebrows became long and symmetrically curved down into the line of the slightly aquiline nose. The sculpture became very refined, and details such as the jewellery usually worn by the Bodhisattvas were minutely represented.

Later in the Nara period further styles evolved. The Tempyō era (729–49), in particular, lends its name to figures surviving in the Kōfukuji and other Nara temples. China was at a high point of prosperity under the T'ang government, and Japan came under its influence in all fields of art. Music and drama were imported and adopted by the Nara court. Rich goods were brought from far distant lands, including textiles, glass and metalwork brought from as far away as Persia by the overland Silk Road through China. Among the deities first adopted in Japan during the Tempyō era are many with features and styles of dress deriving from India or even further west. Deities originating in pre-Buddhist India, some partly animal or with several arms, were introduced. Images of clay, popular first in India and then in T'ang China, were first made during the period. The dynamic clay figures of the Four Heavenly Guardians in the Kōfukuji Temple were later to provide inspiration for the sculptors of the Kamakura period (no. 12).

Such figures were built up on a framework of wood, sometimes packed with straw. They were either wholly or partially painted after drying. As paint sinks into the clay and does not give a smooth surface with a bright appearance, the figures were sometimes covered in lacquer and gilded, and the eyes were sometimes made of obsidian. Clay was used mostly in the Nara period but was revived during the Kamakura period, particularly in temples of the Zen sects. A method of manufacture which made possible light and durable figures became widespread, known as *kanshitsu*. In this method layers of hemp soaked in lacquer were built up over a clay base, rather like papier mâché. The clay core could be removed after the lacquer had set hard, either through a hole in the base, or by withdrawing it through a hole made by cutting out a section of the back, which could then be replaced. Clay and *kanshitsu* were little used after the Nara period. Bronze and wood, however, continued as the basic materials for sculpture until the mid-nineteenth century.

Heian period (AD 794–1185)

The capital was moved from Nara in 784 for a brief ten years to Nagaoka, and then in 794 to Heiankyo, present-day Kyoto. The moves were compelled by arguments of succession and so that the court could escape from the powerful influences exerted over it by the monks of Nara. Indeed, the court took care to ensure that, with the exception of two great temples, the Tōji in the east and the Saiji in the west of Kyoto, there were no longer any temples built within the capital which might house armed communities of monks like those of Nara. The Chinese political system of state ownership of land and central control gradually gave way to a growing feudal system, with several clans vying for power. Chinese influence remained strong in sculpture until diplomatic relations were broken off in 838 and Japan isolated herself politically for a period of 300 years.

During this time society and the arts developed largely under the influence of the aristocracy and of the Buddhist temples. The Japanese had in the late sixth century adopted the written characters used in China and gradually developed versions of them more suited to their temperament. The Heian period produced great works of secular literature, novels and poetry. The Fujiwara family became the most influential of the great clans, providing ministers of government and wives for the royal princes. They patronised the arts and religion. During the Heian period, under the influence of the Buddhist practice of venerating images of the deities, their Shintō counterparts were sometimes represented in sculpture or painting as male and female Japanese aristocratic figures, with expressions and features far removed from the Chinese style of older images.

In the early Heian period two monks who had studied in China, Kūkai, or Kōbō Daishi (774–835), and Saichō, or Dengyō Daishi (767–822), respectively introduced two sects of Mikkyō, or esoteric Buddhism, the Shingon and Tendai. The teachings of esoteric Buddhism included the mystical use of instruments, the contemplation of diagrammatic pictorial schemes of the various aspects of existence (called *mandalas*), the chanting of *sutras*, and the injection in religious ceremony of sound and colour as further aids to inducing a state of awareness. Human emotions and passions were given visual forms which originated as the Myō-Ō in Indian Tantric Buddhism. Tendai professed the way to enlightenment through contemplation of three aspects of existence, the void, the absolute and the temporary, and held that the whole of existence is contained in the minutest part of it. The deities venerated by the new sects were stranger than the guardian figures of the Tempyō period. The central figure is Dainichi Nyorai, the Buddha of Boundless Light. Others are the Bodhisattva Jizō, the guardian Bishamon, various Myō-Ō, and the twelve Bushu. The Myō-Ō, or Kings of Light, strange figures with blue bodies and ferocious expressions, each representing a subject for contemplation, are seen for the first time. Some of the deities, like the eleven-headed Kannon, whose Bodhisattva head is surmounted by ten Nyorai heads, and the thousand-armed Kannon, had been introduced during the Nara period, but without the relevant *sutras* their meaning was hardly understood.

The esoteric sects at first flourished under the sponsorship of the aristocracy. Magical aspects of Mikkyō, particularly the exorcism rituals, had affinities with Shintō practice. Yet their concepts were difficult to grasp, and progress towards understanding was by deep involvement in the rituals. The more readily comprehensible Pure Land (Jōdo) sects also began to take hold of people's minds. They saw Amida, the Buddha who rules the Western Paradise, as a munificent figure who granted eternal salvation to those who believe in him. Amida is often accompanied by the two Bodhisattvas Kannon and Seishi, who assist him by direct intervention in human affairs. Many found the principles of this Amidaism attractive, hoping to enjoy the pleasure of the Western Paradise after death much as they enjoyed the pleasure of their life on earth. Theologians like Ennin in the ninth century and the monks Genshin and Kuya (903–72) spread the Pure Land teaching through Japan, but during the Heian period Buddhism was never really available to the agricultural masses, and the joyful teachings of Jōdo did not gain momentum among them until the Kamakura period.

The faces of the Jōdo Buddhist images in this period look kind and gentle, expressing the idea of a safe haven for the believer. A style of architecture imitating the vision of the Western Paradise provided in the houses of the aristocracy their own hall of worship and holy image. A prevalent belief in a concept called Mappō, which claimed the degradation of the human race and the end of the Buddhist law were to commence in the year 1052, further strengthened the need for such a powerful form of salvation. The Byōdōin at Uji near Kyoto was built in 1053 as a mansion for Fujiwara Yorimitsu in this style. Inside the central hall is a figure of Amida Nyorai made by the sculptor Jōchō (d. 1057), among whose successors were most of the prominent sculptors of the Kamakura period. The figure shows something of the grace of the Tempyō era sculpture (AD 729–48), in contrast to the ponderously authoritative works which were produced in the ninth century during the expansion of Mikkyō. Both the mansion and the Amida figure indicate the comfortable warmth of the Heian period ideal. But the Fujiwara style of the Amida and Bodhisattva figures was to persist into the Kamakura period as a major influence on the spread of Amidaism among the common people. Its influence can be seen particularly in the work of the sculptor Kaikei who was himself an ardent Pure Land devotee (no. 14).

In contrast to the clay, cast-bronze and *kanshitsu* modelling of images prevalent during the Nara period, Heian period statues are almost entirely carved from wood. Since the usual method was *ichiboku zukuri*, or sculpture from a single block, the early Heian pieces tend to be smaller than those of the Nara period. Techniques of sculpture developed, however, and by the end of the period the method of *yosegi zukuri*, whereby the image was formed from a number of carved pieces fitted together, was already in widespread use.

Wood sculpture – techniques and materials

Japan had an already thriving tradition in the use of wood in architecture, and a deep understanding of the problems involved in its use by the time Buddhism was introduced. Wood had to be seasoned so that it would not warp or crack under the effect of the extreme changes in temperature and humidity experienced in Japan. In order to reduce the effect of stresses within the timber, logs containing the heart of the tree were rarely used as main structural components, and it was more usual to work with a half- or quarter-section of a tree-trunk. A further precaution in architecture was to make longitudinal cuts along beams and pillars to take up any expansion or contraction. The components were then arranged so that the cuts would be concealed. The same problem was treated in a similar way with the earliest wood sculpture, which was carved from a solid block in the method known as *ichiboku zukuri*.

During the Asuka period several different woods, from both coniferous and deciduous trees, were used for sculpture, some of which were fragrant and some of which were naturally coloured. But in the Nara and Heian periods the cypress became the preferred material, because of its fragrance, whiteness, texture and smoothness of grain, and remained the favourite until the mid-nineteenth century. The choice of wood was not just a matter of materials, for trees themselves were considered holy, some being regarded as manifestations of Shintō gods. This might explain the preponderance of solid-block construction in Shintō sculpture even after the widespread change to hollow sculpture during the Kamakura period, since the centre of the image could be considered to house, in a sense, the spirit of the tree. Sometimes groups of related deities were carved from the same tree, presumably so that the same spirit should pervade them.

Japanese sculptors found no difficulty in thus combining Shintō and Buddhist sensibilities, just as Shintō shrines and Buddhist temples were often allowed to occupy the same precinct in a symbiotic relationship.

Ichiboku zukuri and yosegi zukuri

As already mentioned, most early wood sculpture was carved from a single block, sometimes with limbs made separately. The block was carefully selected usually avoiding the heartwood. The earliest pieces of sculpture in Japan illustrate the degree of sophistication necessary in the selection of the block. An example is the seventh-century figure of Miroku in the Kōryūji Temple of Kyoto. The figure sits in the posture known as *hanka*, with one leg supported across the other knee and with the upper body arched forward. A log with a suitable curve was selected, and the figure carved from a segment of it, so that the original heart of the tree lay on an imaginary curve drawn in front of the figure. The fear of splitting at critical places was further reduced by cutting hollows into the back, behind the head and behind the left knee. A further sophistication, and precursor of the perfected *yosegi zukuri* method common on work of the eleventh and twelfth centuries, was to split the block vertically across, scooping out the inside and rejoining it along the original lines of the split. When the head and torso are carved from the same block, the narrow neck section exposes different layers of wood from the wider head and shoulders and deformation is likely. To prevent the neck from thus warping, the head is first removed by cutting obliquely inward around the base of the neck. The hollow which results from the removal of the neck can be continued into the cavity in the body. The head is replaced and held by slivers of wood to adjust the angle and hold it firm.

Using a single block places a limit on the size of the finished work, with the additional risk of residual stresses causing cracks to occur. The final solution was *yosegi zukuri*, which consisted of building the figure out of a number of smaller blocks hollowed and carved, then jointed together. Most of the components could be carved separately by a group of craftsmen under the direction of a master sculptor to produce a large figure with a relatively thin wall of wood. As a number of people could work on each statue, the learning process must have been accelerated and the growth of the sculpture guilds promoted. Some images were sculpted so thin that the wall was accidentally penetrated by the chisel, so that repairs had to be made by inserting more wood from the inside. The removal of the size limitation imposed by the single-block method enabled the manufacture of much larger figures, around five metres high, known as *jōroku butsu*. The word *jōroku* describes the height, which is 1 *jō* and *roku* (6) *shaku*. There are 10 *shaku* in 1 *jō* (1 *shaku* = 30.3 cm approx.). A form of *yosegi* was perfected in the Heian period by Jōchō and by the late twelfth century had become the normal method for wood sculpture.

Hollow sculptures of the Kamakura period sometimes have a shelf inserted inside the body on which devotional objects could be placed to be sealed inside the image. Inserted *sutras* or other documents have yielded much information on dating in recent years, when pieces have been dismantled as part of conservation work.

Gyokugan

In addition to the freedom afforded the sculptor by the *yosegi zukuri* technique, the impact of Kamakura period sculpture owes much to the uniquely Japanese method of making the eyes using pieces of shaped crystal – *gyokugan* – inserted into the open eye sockets from behind and fixed in place using bamboo pins. The pupils are painted in black, and the whites of the eyes simulated by stretching either silk or paper across the back. Eyes made in this way appear deep and seem to move in the flickering light of temple lamps. Their effect in their original gloomy settings must have been dramatic.

The renaissance movement and the Kei school

The renaissance of Japanese sculpture during the Kamakura period occurred partly through a renewed interest in China after the three centuries of comparative isolation, partly through the spread of the Pure Land sect among the common people, and partly because of the change to the feudal government of samurai at Kamakura.

The first images to be made during the period in the old eighth-century Tempyō style, which had been strongly influenced by T'ang dynasty China, followed the burning of the Kōfukuji and Tōdaiji Temples of Nara by Taira Shigehira in 1180, during the later stages of the Gempei war. The destroyed Nanendō hall of the Kōfukuji Temple had been built originally in 814 by Fujiwara Fuyutsugu, and the temple was accordingly considered the family temple of the Fujiwaras. Both the Kōfukuji and the Tōdaiji had been sympathetic towards the Fujiwara who had supported the Minamoto during the wars. After the fire it was Fujiwara Kanezane who had the Nanendō rebuilt. Kanezane became the leading member of the committee of ten appointed aristocrats whose job was to represent the wishes of the Kamakura government to the aristocracy of Kyoto. He appointed the local sculptor Kōkei to replace several images of the Tempyō period which had been lost in the fire, thus contributing to the renaissance of the energetic Tempyō style. Minamoto Yoritomo and his newly formed military government at Kamakura not only supported the restoration of the temples but were also themselves deeply involved in the practice and dissemination of Buddhism.

Kōkei was one of the *busshi* of Nara, a guild of specialist sculptors of wooden Buddhist images, whose lineage extended back to Jōchō (d. 1057) of Kyoto. Seichō, the head of the school, had persuaded the authorities that the Nara school should be given the commissions for the work on the Nanendō in preference over their rivals, Myōen (d. 1199) and Inson

(d. 1198) of Kyoto, who were responsible for the greater part of the temples' reconstruction. The Kei school, so named because the syllable *kei* occurs in the names of its most prominent sculptors, became the mainstream among the several schools of sculpture which flourished during the period. Unkei, Kōkei's natural son, and Kaikei, his beloved pupil, matured to become the greatest of Japanese sculptors. The renaissance movement spread to the Kyoto schools, and the descendants of Myōen and Inson were later to make sculpture not dissimilar to that of the Kei school, although preserving their separate identity during the period of Kamakura government.

From 1188 Kōkei worked on replacements of the lost sculptures of the Fukukenzaku Kannon, the principal deity, the six figures of the patriarchs of the Hossō sect, and the images of the Four Guardian Kings in the Nanendō hall of the Kōfukuji Temple. Among them the huge figure of Tamon Ten, Guardian of the South (no. 2), is perhaps one of the most representative sculptures of the early renaissance movement. It is basically in the Tempyō style of guardian deities yet shows a dynamism in the deep carving of both the body and garment, and a sense of immediate movement in the limbs, altogether typical of the spirit of the new age. Kōkei's figures of the six patriarchs are similarly highly naturalistic. Each has a strongly individual expression and sits in a different pose. The faces are lined and wrinkled, with veins standing out prominently. The eyes are of inset crystal which distinguishes Kamakura period work.

Chinese influence

The old ties with China which had been loosened during the 300 years of the Fujiwara period were resumed during the late twelfth century. Priests visited China eager for learning, and Chinese artists were made welcome in Japan. Chinese coinage was imported and used as currency in Japan, as it had been also in the T'ang period. Itinerant salesmen purveyed Chinese herbal medicine in towns and countryside, acquiring their goods through the monasteries. Even today temples like the Zenkōji in Nagano have a traditional connection with the medicine industry. Paintings of the Song dynasty were prized. Calligraphy and Buddhist paintings were brought from China by monks like Shunjo (1166–1277) to inspire Japanese painters and sculptors. Certain features of Chinese art became a normal part of Kamakura period imagery. Bodhisattvas were depicted with elevated hair arrangements and wearing pierced and jewelled gilt-bronze crowns with hanging decorative side-pieces. Their robes swirled about their limbs imparting a vivid sense of movement. The sleeves hung low below the hands, which had the long finely manicured fingernails of the Chinese aristocracy. The technique used in painting of applying gold foil over a white pigment-backed silk was adapted for the decoration of the garments of sculptures. Decorative roundels of grasses and flowers made of moulded clay pieces were applied to garments, adding to the vividness of the figures. Chinese furniture, like the high-backed chairs on which priests are often shown sitting (no. 32), was used, particularly in the Zen monasteries.

Prominent among those with a deep interest in China was the monk Shunjōbō Chōgen (1122–1206), who was appointed supervisor over the reconstruction of the Tōdaiji Temple after the fire of 1180. Chōgen was a keen exponent of Chinese thinking and styles in art and architecture. He had been to China three times and brought back with him Song dynasty Buddhist paintings which were hung in his *besshō* (local headquarters) in various parts of Japan. Paintings such as these were the models for the sculptors of the Kei school. The close working relationship between the sculptor Kaikei and Chōgen is indicated in the *Namu Amida Butsu Sagyō Chō* which records that an Amida triad made for the *besshō* at Harima (the Jōdoji) and sculpture in the *besshō* at Iga (the Shin Daibutsuji) were made by Kaikei with reference to Chinese paintings. Chōgen had further employed a bronze founder from China to oversee the repair of the melted head and hand of the great bronze figure of Biroshana in the Tōdaiji in preference to a Japanese craftsman, indicating the extent to which the new ways had taken a grip on society. He also introduced the Tenjiku style in architecture from China. Both the Daibutsuden hall for the great seated figure of Birushana (Japan's largest) and the Nandaimon gate which houses the two huge wooden Kongō Rikishi made by Unkei and Kaikei are in this style.

Unkei

Unkei's earliest known sculpture is a figure of Dainichi Nyorai made in 1175 for the Enjōji Temple in Nara, at a time when he was presumably still working largely under the guidance of his father, Kōkei. An inscription on the figure tells that the sculptor was Unkei, the 'True pupil of Kōkei'. The figure shows a vigour wholly in keeping with the coming renaissance in sculpture and already illustrates the influence of Chinese Song dynasty art, with the light flowing garment, high hair arrangement and decoratively pierced gilt metal crown.

In 1186 Unkei was in eastern Japan, making sculptures for the Ganjōjūin Temple, which had been built by Yoritomo's father-in-law, Hōjō Tokimasa, and in 1189 for the Jōrakuji Temple in Sagami. The head of the Nara school, Seichō, had also been invited to the east in 1185 by the Shogun to make a *jōroku*-size figure (see p. 29) of Amida Nyorai for the Shōchōjuin Temple. For the Jōrakuji Unkei made a triad of a figure of Amida with two attendant Bodhisattvas, plus figures of Bishamon Ten and Fudō Myō-Ō. The style of the Jōrakuji Bodhisattvas is very similar to a Bodhisattva (no. 3) in the nearby Manganji Temple, which can therefore be confidently attributed to the work of Unkei. The Chinese style of the hair tied up high on the head, the downward cast of the upper eyelids and the fluidity of the robes recall the style of Unkei's earlier 1175 figure of

Dainichi Nyorai. Similar characteristics are evident also on the figure of
Taishaku Ten (no. 4) from the Takisanji Temple in Aichi Prefecture, also
believed to be by Unkei or a colleague close to him, although the pigments
on the piece are of a later date.

Unkei returned from the Kamakura area to continue work together
with his father. In 1193 he was honoured with the Buddhist title of
Hokkyō ('Bridge of the Law'). He probably replaced his father as head of
the Nara busshi in 1195, since in that year Kōkei relinquished his own
Buddhist title of Hōgen ('Eye of the Law') in favour of his son. In the
following year Kōkei and Unkei worked on the attendant figure of the
Bodhisattva Kokuzō for the great bronze statue of Biroshana in the Tōdaiji.
Unkei's brother Jōkaku and Kōkei's leading pupil Kaikei made the other
attendant figure of the Bodhisattva Nyoirin Kannon. The four sculptors
each made one of the Four Heavenly Guardians which were placed to the
north, south, east and west of the Biroshana.

In 1197 Unkei was in Kyoto, where he worked on the repair of the
Heian period sculptures in the Tōji and other temples. He made two Ni-Ō
figures and a group of eight demonic deities, the Yasha, for the Jingoji
Temple high in the mountains outside Kyoto. The adventurous style of this
period in his life is well represented by Kongara Dōji (no. 5) from a group
of the eight dōji acolytes of Fudō Myō-Ō which he made for the Fudō hall
in the Kongōbuji Temple on Mount Kōya to accompany the main deity,
Fudō Myō-Ō. The sculptor felt free to add a light-hearted touch to his work,
since the dōji did not have to be treated with the solemnity due to higher
deities. The richness and warmth of the flesh and the intensity in the
youthful expression make a lasting impression of immediate humanity.

Both Unkei and his father are known to have worked on the immense
project of the manufacture of the thousand and one figures of the Senjū
Kannon, or thousand-armed Kannon, in the Sanjūsangendō hall of the
Myōhōin Temple in Kyoto. One of the figures has the name Unkei inscribed
on it and is markedly similar to his early Dainichi figure in the Enjōji
Temple.

The best known of all Unkei's work is probably the eight and a half
metre high figure of the Ni-Ō, Naraen Kongō, made in 1203 in a period
of just seventy days. Unkei's colleague Kaikei made the other figure of the
pair, Misshaku Kongō, which guard the main gate of the Tōdaiji Temple.
The two muscular sculptures have angry expressions, and their postures
and violent movement, together with the swirl of their lower garments,
must have made them seem almost alive to the people of Nara.
Interestingly the figures were carved lying horizontally, for when they
were erected Unkei was dissatisfied with the direction of the gaze and the
proportions of the Naraen figure. He had the eyes altered, the height of
the waist adjusted, and an extra block of wood fixed to the upper arm so
that he could carve a larger muscle. The Misshaku, which was the work
of Kaikei, is slightly more delicately carved, and had no last-minute

changes made to it. The figures were probably well known to the sculptor who made the Ni-Ō (no. 1) who guard the gate of the Nakayamadera Temple in Fukui Prefecture and, although not on the immense scale of the Tōdaiji figures, show a similar vigour and ferocity which are characteristic of early thirteenth-century work.

Unkei's prestige grew and he settled in Kyoto where he worked with his six sons on projects like the Ni-Ō figures for the south gate of the Tōji Temple in 1209. He was honoured with the title Dai Busshi ('Master Sculptor') by the temple. Perhaps Unkei's greatest pieces are the masterly portraits of Muchaku and Seshin, the founder patriarchs of the Hossō sect for the Hokuendō of the Kōfukuji Temple made between 1208 and 1212. The figures have a character and life of their own, far more vivid than the Nanendō pieces by Unkei's father made about twenty years previously. The figures are made from three vertical pieces, hollowed out but leaving a thick wall into which the robes and features are deeply and confidently carved. The humane postures and facial expressions are far removed from the ethereal iconographic styles which Unkei replaced, and might be said to indicate his maturity and the height of his spiritual development. Unkei died in 1223 at an advanced age.

Kaikei

The work of Unkei shows unmistakable influence from Chinese Song dynasty (960–1279) Buddhist art, but many of his sculptures are a vigorous interpretation of the Tempyō era style. However, Kaikei, his elder and fellow pupil of Kōkei, seems to have gone a stage further, and in addition to the two styles developed a fusion of the Song and the gentle Fujiwara styles, to produce sweet-faced Buddhas and Bodhisattvas which became the ideal of the Pure Land sect.

A passionate Pure Land devotee, Kaikei had many close friends in the priesthood, among them Chōgen. From Chōgen Kaikei received the Buddhist name An-amidabutsu, and signed his work thus, with the first syllable 'An' written in Sanskrit. In his early period he was also known as Tamba Kosho Kaikei, or just Busshi Kaikei. More than twenty sculptures by Kaikei are known, although he made many more during his lifetime which have been lost. Among his earliest-known works is the figure of the Bodhisattva Miroku, now in Boston Museum of Fine Arts, which was made for the Kōfukuji Temple in 1189. It is possible to date Kaikei's sculpture roughly by his method of signing. In the decade or so before 1203 he signed An-amidabutsu, Kosho Kaikei, or Busshi Kaikei, but in that year he was awarded the Buddhist title Hokkyō and signed his work accordingly. He was later, probably between 1208 and 1210, awarded the rank Hōgen.

Kaikei's work in the Tempyō style contains perhaps more of the classical element than that of Unkei. He consciously built on the tradition in the same way that he continued to develop the Heian period aristocratic

Detail of no. I, Kongō Rikishi (Ungyō)

interpretation of Pure Land images. The two military deities Shukongō Shin and Jinja Taishō (no. 12) from the Kongōin, Kyoto, show this less dynamic contribution by Kaikei to the renaissance. The Shukongō Shin is a version of a Tempyō era clay figure in the Hokkedō hall of the Tōdaiji Temple. Compared with the guardian Tamon Ten (no. 2) by Kaikei's teacher Kōkei, which has a similar military dress, the tunic is relatively static and shows little sign of the realistic Song style treatment of the established Kei school. The strange figure of Jinja Taishō is thought to have been inspired by a Heian period esoteric Buddhist painting. However, the intensity of both figures, and particularly the treatment of the muscles and tendons on the Jinja Taishō, show the underlying strength of the sculptor's style. A further development of Kaikei's intensity of expression is shown by the figure of the attendant on the Bodhisattva Monju Bosatsu, Zenzai Dōji, from the Monjuin, Nara (no. 13). The figure has a somewhat unnervingly mature expression for the youthfulness of the subject (cf. no. 11), indicating perhaps the sculptor's own self-confidence and the depth of his understanding of the various aspects of Buddhism. The robes of this figure, and the posture in movement, are far stronger than the delicate style of the Song, although clearly deriving from it.

Kaikei's Pure Land style reached a maturity in the first decade of the thirteenth century, in a final Japanisation of the Song style. The standing figure of the Bodhisattva Jizō from the Hokkedō hall in the Tōdaiji Temple (no.14) is typical of the perfected Kaikei style and can be closely dated to within the years 1203 and 1210 by the Hokkyō signature. The Bodhisattva is shown in his common guise of a monk and wears a rich necklace and garment decorated with cut gold foil falling in long, light folds in a subdued development of the Song style. The features reflect Chinese influence in the long almond-shaped eyes and an aristocratic fullness around the mouth, but the expression is a fusion of the softness of the Fujiwara Pure Land ideal and the features of an ordinary Japanese priest. This idealised image with its sweet facial expression was perpetuated by Kaikei's followers, although the sternness which characterises the Kamakura period is also evident on later works of his school, like the standing Amida by his pupil Gyōkai (no. 16), made in 1253 for the Amidaji Temple of Shiga Prefecture. Kaikei's later works exhibit a further degree of naturalism and humanisation in smaller sculptures, such as no. 15.

The sons and apprentices of Unkei

Unkei had six sons, and sculpture by only three of them – Kōsho, Kōben and Tankei – survives. The work of Tankei (1173–1256) was closest to that of his father. In particular, he inherited and continued Unkei's dramatic style, but his work is individual and in no way that of a mere copyist. He worked with Unkei on various projects until his father's death but also made sculpture in his own right. In 1229 he made figures of the deities Byakkō Shin and Zenmyō Shin (no. 8) for the Kōzanji Temple,

Kyoto, in his own individual quiet interpretation of the Song style.

Tankei's most representative work is the great figure of the Senju Kannon of *jōroku* proportions in the Sanjūsangendō hall in the Myōhōin, Kyoto, which was made between 1251 and 1254 following the loss of the original in a fire in 1249, together with several signed pieces among the thousand smaller versions of the Bodhisattvas in that temple building. Two extraordinary figures of the wind and thunder deities, Fujin and Raijin, and some of the twenty-eight Bushu, are thought to have been made by him together with his brothers Kōben and Kōsho. A version of one of these twenty-eight figures, that of Basu Sennin, made by the sculptor Eiken in 1308 (no. 26), appears to owe much to the Myōhōin piece and indicates the extent of the influence of the Kei school right through the Kamakura period. As the eldest son of Unkei, Tankei inherited the Shichijō Busshō (the sculpture studio on the Shichijō street of Kyoto). He died at the age of eighty-three while still active.

Other sculptors are known to have been members of the Kei school during the early decades of the thirteenth century, although details of their lives and lineages are lacking. The Amida triad (no. 7), from Kuwabara Ku in Shizuoka Prefecture, signed Jikei can be dated to the late twelfth century and attributed to Unkei's studio from stylistic considerations. Another sculptor of the Kei school, Renkei, made the figure of Kichijō Ten (no. 9) in the Fukkōonji Temple, Yamanashi Prefecture. The female deity is given a rather masculine air, reflecting perhaps the spirit of this military age.

The sons and disciples of Unkei's sons continued with the naturalistic sculpture movement. Unkei's grandson Kōen was the son of Kōun and nephew to Tankei under whom he worked on the Sanjūsangendō from 1251 until Tankei's death in 1254. He inherited the leadership of the Sanjūsangendō project until 1266, himself making several of the thousand figures of the Senjū Kannon. In the following year he made the four attendants (no. 10) of the Four Heavenly Guardian figures in the Shingondō in the Eikyūji Temple in Nara. The humorous treatment of the figures, with their expressions of human weakness and doubt, is reminiscent of earlier sculpture of the Kei school, particularly the lantern-carrying demons Ryutoki and Tentoki made by Kōen's uncle, Kōben, for the Kōfukuji Temple in Nara in 1215. Kōen's particular approach to realism is further well exemplified by the group of the Bodhisattva Monju and four attendants (no. 11) made in 1273 for the Kōfukuji Temple. The figure of Monju has an unworldly beauty common to Kei school Bodhisattvas, yet the realism of the attendants is close to an ordinariness with which common people could readily identify. The pieces reveal the down-to-earth side of Buddhism during the late Kamakura period.

The Kei school descended originally from the studio of Jōchō (d.1057), the earliest specialist sculptor of wooden Buddhist images whose work survives; he was active in Kyoto under the sponsorship of the Fujiwaras.

Detail of no. 26

Although the capital had moved from Nara to Kyoto at the end of the eighth century, the influential Fujiwaras retained strong links with the Nara temples and shrines like their family temple, the Kōfukuji. So when in 1096 the Kōfukuji was burnt to the ground it was natural that the Fujiwara should commission those same sculptors whom they patronised in Kyoto to reconstruct the statuary of the temple.

Raijō, the grandson of Jōchō, was chosen to replace the Nara period figures which had been lost, and his son Kōjō settled in Nara as the first of the line of *busshi* from which the Kamakura period Kei school descended. There was accordingly a long established and continuing tradition of replacement and repair of Nara period sculpture by the school of Kōkei when the Tōdaiji and Kōfukuji Temples were destroyed. The immediate successors to Kōkei were Unkei and his six sons Tankei, Kōben, Kōun, Kōsho, Unjō and Unga. Kaikei and his pupils Gyōkai, Eikai and Chōkai are usually considered a separate branch of the school because Kaikei's individual style is so distinctive. Two further important sculptors were Jōkei I and Jōkei II, who worked on projects associated with the Kei school. The relationship between Jōkei I and Jōkei II is not known, although it has been suggested that Jōkei I, whose Kongō Rikishi in the Kōfukuji many regard as the epitome of Kamakura period sculpture, was one of Unkei's sons working under an alternative name. It seems there were other sculptors signing Jōkei who worked in the late Kamakura period, but they are not known to be related to the Kei school. Jōkei II, who was entitled Higo Betto Jōkei, outstripped Kaikei in the fine execution of intricate folds, high, complex hair-styles, and elegant hanging necklaces and other jewellery deriving from Song painting styles. Those characteristics on the Nyoirin Kannon (no. 17) from the Tōgenji Temple in Kyoto, which is dated to 1256, identify the work as that of a close pupil of Jōkei II.

Work by Kōkei's grandsons, Kōen (nos 10, 11), Kōsei and Kōshun, and from the pupils of Kaikei of the same generation, Gyōkai (no. 16), Eikai and Chōkai, survives. Their styles became universal among sculptors during the Kamakura period, including the old Kyoto studios. An immense pair of Ni-Ō figures over five metres high were made in 1338 for the Kimpusenji Temple near Nara by Kōsei, the son of Kōshun and great-grandson of Kōkei, in a rugged style, which although forceful and typically Kamakura period, lack the combination of elegance and vitality of the work of Unkei's time. The Kamakura government fell in 1333 and the city was sacked, to be followed by three-quarters of a century of civil war before the nation became again, for a short while, sufficiently stable to accommodate such large-scale temple enterprises. Records of the Kei school from this time are sparse, although the style continued right through to the Edo period. Despite the relative decline in Buddhist sculptural art after the Kamakura period, a continuity of style is evident, for example, in a pair of figures of the Bodhisattvas Fugen and Monju mounted on an elephant and a *shishi* in the collection of the British Museum (JA 1988,3–14,1–2). These figures were made in the early seventeenth century by a sculptor, Kōyū, whose name includes the same character *kō* used in the name of Kōkei and the sons and grandsons of Unkei.

Other schools

Among the sculptors influenced by the Kei school were the Zen school, similarly so called after the use of the character *zen* in their individual names. They were leading sculptors in Nara after Unkei had removed to the Shichijō studio in Kyoto. The Zen school sculptors, chiefly Zenen, Zenkei and his son Zenshun, had a special relationship with the Saidaiji Temple, for which they made several images. Among them are a copy by Zenkei in 1249 of the Shaka Nyorai in the Seiryōji Temple, which had been brought originally from China by Chōnen in the tenth century (cf. no. 18, another version of the same statue by Inho in the Shōmyōji Temple). A seated figure of Eison of the Risshū sect, made when the priest was seventy-nine years old in 1280, by Zeshun in the Saidaiji remains one of the greatest portraits of the period and one of the last great works of the school.

In Kyoto the En school made Fujiwara-style sculptures for the aristocracy. This was a group centred on Chōsei, a pupil of Jōchō. The successor of Chōsei was named Enso, and later generations used the character *en* in their names. They are known as the Sanjō Busshō group, since their studio was situated in the Sanjō street of Kyoto, but although well established their reputation was eclipsed after Unkei opened his own studio in Shichijō street, and also following the death of the leader of the school, Myōen, in 1199.

When Raijō went to Nara in 1096 to work on the restoration of the Kōfukuji Temple, a fellow pupil of Kakujō, named Injō, remained in Kyoto. Like the En school, the followers of Injō worked during the late Heian period mainly for the aristocracy, producing refined and gentle pieces in the contemporary 'Japanese' style. Members of the school worked together with the Kei school on projects like the restoration of the Tōdaiji and Kōfukuji Temples at the end of the twelfth century. They remained in close contact with them after the death of Inson in 1198 in Kyoto, when the school succumbed to the greater power of Unkei's Shichijō studio, as had their fellows of the En school after the death of Myōen. Members of the In school, including their leader, Inkei, worked on the great Sanjūsangendō projects between 1251 and 1266, and unlike the En school they preserved their separate identity to a considerable extent through to the late Kamakura period. A number of sculptors of the school under Inho made the important Shōmyōji Temple version of the Seiryōji figure of Shaka Nyorai (no. 18) as late as 1308, showing the continuity of their weightily confident style. There were still In school sculptors active around Kamakura after the decline of the Kei school.

The influence of the sects of Buddhism

Buddhism spread rapidly among the lower classes through the efforts of evangelical priests like Nichiren Shōnin (1222–82) who, unusually, attacked all other sects of Buddhism, holding that the whole truth is revealed in the Lotus *Sūtra*. He attracted a huge following, and his portrait (sculptural or painted) was venerated in temples of the sect after his death, but the influence of Nichiren Buddhism was otherwise not very great on the visual arts.

More importantly, various sects of Pure Land Buddhism spread during the Kamakura period among all classes of people but especially with the agricultural population, to whom Buddhism had been not very accessible during the Heian period. They were all based upon belief in the fulfilment of forty-eight vows made by Amida Nyorai, Lord of the Western Paradise, who offers salvation to those who sincerely invoke him. The major creeds of Amidaism were the Yuzu Nembutsu, founded by Ryōnin (1073–1132), the Jōdo (Pure land) sect propagated by Honen (1133–1212), the Jōdo Shinshū of Shinran (1173–1263) and the Jishū sect of Ippen (1239–89).

Although Pure Land became the most popular form of Buddhism during the Kamakura period, it had in fact been known in Japan since the early Nara period. Ritual like the Neri Kuyo, an annual masked processional drama illustrating the Bodhisattva's leading the soul of the deceased to Amida's Pure Land, had been enacted at temples like the Taema-den since the eighth century. The popularity of the Pure Land doctrine among the nobility during the Fujiwara period had ensured that there should be a thriving tradition of sculpture of Amida accomplished by Bodhisattva attendants, exemplified by the work of Jōchō, the distant ancestor of the Kei school. Many temples were built, each with a main image of Amida with attendants, and the influence of Jōchō's 'Fujiwara' style remained throughout the period in the work of the Kei school (no. 7) and the traditional schools of Kyoto.

The mass movement towards Amidaism in the Kamakura period was on a scale which might be compared with the enthusiastic period of temple building in the Nara period under the Emperor Shōmu. As Shōmu had built the sixteen-metre-high bronze figure of Birushana in the Tōdaiji in the eighth century, so in 1252 a seated bronze Amida of equally impressive dimensions was constructed at the Kōtokuin in Kamakura. Although strictly an esoteric form of Amida, its calm dignity remains witness to the influence of Zen on its military sponsors – for, together with the various Pure Land sects, the most significant and energetic movement which gripped the military clans during the Kamakura period was Zen (Dhyana). Zen is said to have been brought from India to China in the sixth century by Daruma (Bodhidharma). Rinzai Zen was introduced into Japan by the monk Eisai (1141—1215) of the esoteric Tendai sect, at a time when it was flourishing in the monasteries around the capital of Song

China. The essence of the teaching is to see directly into the true nature of things mainly through meditation, and although belief and dogma were respected, they were to be transcended by the individual through his own spiritual endeavours. The Japanese took the Chinese connection between the study of Rinzai and the arts, particularly painting and calligraphy, a step further, and it became the focus of the moral education of the military class.

Shintō, which had been nurse to all professions, arts and crafts since before the introduction of Buddhism in the sixth century AD, provided the structure whereby Zen could become infused into secular activities in Japan. Zen became an essential part of military training, and schools of archery and swordplay developed into physical exercises designed to promote spiritual progress, in a way reminiscent of the use of ritual and paraphernalia in esoteric Buddhism. The drinking of tea was practised to promote alertness during periods of contemplation. The Tea Ceremony, which became established as a distinct art in the fifteenth century under the patronage of the Ashikaga Shoguns, has its Japanese origins in the Zen temples of the thirteenth century. Although Zen is sometimes now thought of as a kind of abstract philosophy, it is in essence identical in spirit with the original teachings of the historic Buddha. In fact, the Mahāyāna concept that enlightenment is possible for all beings brought closer those Bodhisattvas and other deities which had achieved levels of enlightenment attainable also to human beings through the practice of Zen, and the great monks of the religion themselves were accordingly venerated even more than the images of the deities in their temples. A further branch, Soto Zen, which laid emphasis on seated meditation, was introduced by the monk Dōgen (1200–53). He was the first abbot of the Eiheiji Temple in the frontier province of Echizen, high in the mountains and thus far removed from the worldly intrigues which had ridden Buddhism during the Nara and Heian periods.

Since Zen aims at the direct knowledge of the Buddha nature, Shaka Nyorai himself is especially venerated. But in addition to the traditional images of Buddhas and Bodhisattvas in the main halls of temples, separate halls were built for lectures, study, meditation and personal tutorials. Communities of monks lived in quasi-villages called *tatchū* built near the main monastery structures, in which quiet gardens were laid out to provide an environment for contemplation between the natural and spiritual worlds. The teaching of Zen depends much upon the personal relationship between master and pupil, and the veneration of the master led to the practice of enshrining his image in painted and sculptured portraits both before and after his death. This tendency to humanism is evident in other branches of Buddhism during the Kamakura period, and the personal charisma of the leaders of sects led to their being venerated almost as if they were themselves Buddhas. Indeed, to this day it is popularly supposed that Buddhist believers become enlightened upon

Detail of no. 33

death, and the household shrine dedicated to a deceased parent or other ancestor is always spoken of as housing a Buddha.

Portrait sculpture

Thus the most remarkable innovation during the Kamakura period was the portrayal of contemporary figures in addition to deities, ancestor founders of sects and semi-mythical beings. It was certainly the charisma of the early priests who did so much to spread Buddhism which caused their portraits to be venerated, but the practice was much extended by the Zen sects. Since the essential teachings of Zen are highly personal, and ultimately transmitted by word of mouth directly from master to acolyte, the teaching and indeed the whole life of the master became absorbed by the pupil. This kind of reverence is seen today in the secular world in Japan, and particularly in the traditional schools of arts which have been in the past nurtured in an atmosphere of Zen, such as the Tea Ceremony, flower arrangement and calligraphy.

The lasting monument of Zen to sculpture might be said to be the portrait sculpture of the Kamakura period, when the custom arose of making life-sized images of priests to be kept like the deities themselves in temple halls for veneration after their deaths. The custom then spread to most sects of Buddhism, and portraits of the founders of sects and their main disciples were made and copied for distribution among the temples of each branch. It is in this portraiture that the stark, almost alarming realism of the sculpture of the period is most evident; and in a sense the realism is more than surface deep, for like the images of deities which contain within them *sūtras* and relics, portrait sculptures often contain relics of the subjects themselves.

In eastern Japan especially, where the warrior's ethic had the strongest hold, portraits of the leading Kamakura samurai were made. Some, like that of the Shogun Yoritomo (no. 28) are clothed in formal court attire and might be considered the first secular portraits. Others, like that of Tairako Shigetsune (no. 30), portray the warrior in priest's garb, towards the end of his life. At the end of the Kamakura period another style of priest's portrait, the *chinzō*, became established. The priest sits on a high-backed Chinese-style chair, clad in his everyday robes which hang low over his legs. Although the robes usually lack detail, reflecting the frugality of monastic life and the unimportance of worldly goods, the faces are full of expression, so that an observer might feel the powerful presence of the departed subject (no. 32). This realism at least equals the accurate delineation of features and range of standardised expressions found on much Western art of the later medieval period. The individuality of each priest is always evident, though many examples have an initially rather alarming sternness of expression telling of the austerity of their everyday life. One may speculate to what extent the subject had influence over the sculptor during the creation of these intimate memorials.

Detail of no. 32

The concept of enlightenment by the living, and instant Buddhahood upon death, makes the whole question of whether a portrait is secular or religious rather irrelevant. The purpose of the veneration of the portrait of the master of monk, artisan or tradesman is the same – to preserve and respect the greater wisdom of the past. The widely misunderstood expression of 'ancestor worship', with all its connotations of idolatry to classic monotheists, does an injustice to this most normal of human attitudes.

Revivalist religions and imaginary portraits

This movement towards naturalism found expression in imaginary portraits of founders of a number of revivalist cults from the Nara and Heian periods, some of which were secondary to mainstream Buddhism and some of which became absorbed into it. Certain Buddhist images of venerable pedigree became models for the spread of the faith, and part of the movement away from what the Kamakura military saw as the decadence of the immediate past towards a rediscovery of the original truths of Buddhism. The several compromises between Shintō and Buddhism which had existed in the form of the earlier Ryōbu Shintō movement continued into the Kamakura period. Shintō deities were depicted both with the naturalism of the time and based on archaistic models. The imperial ancestors, with their innate Shintō divinity, obtained status on a par with Buddhist deities, though portraits of them were relatively rare.

Shōtoku Taishi

The Prince Regent Shōtoku Taishi (AD 574–622) is in many ways regarded as the founder of Buddhism in Japan, since it was largely by his endeavours that the first of the great monasteries, the Hōryūji, was built, and he became himself a learned exponent of the *sutras*. A number of legends surrounding his birth and life had grown before the Kamakura period, and he was regarded as having divine status from within a short time of his death. He appears in a variety of forms and identities: for example, in the Nara period the Emperor Shōmu was thought to have been his reincarnation, as was Kūkai (Kōbō Daishi) of the Shingon sect during the Heian period. In the Pure Land sect Shōtoku Taishi was sometimes identified with the Bodhisattva Kannon, and in that form lead the procession which meets the dying believer to escort him or her to Paradise. The Pure Land advocate Shinran is also said to have adopted the faith as a result of a vision of Shōtoku Taishi.

During the Kamakura period the Shōtoku cult spread together with the Pure Land sects to diffuse into all branches of Japanese Buddhism. He became identified with Daruma, the patriarch of Zen. Images of Shōtoku in temples are of several different types, most frequently showing him as a two-year-old making the statement 'Namu Butsu' ('I trust in Buddha', no. 24), as a sixteen-year-old holding a long-handled censor in both hands, praying for the recovery of his sick father, the Emperor Yomei (no. 23), and as a mature statesman.

Rokudō and Emma-Ō

The concept of the Pure Land Paradise for the believer was balanced by a rising preoccupation with the cycles of rebirth for the sinner in the various awful Rokudō, the six worlds of illusion. Upon death the individual's sins were judged by Emma-Ō, the King of Hell, and his or her next stage of existence decided on. The figure originated in Indian scriptures as a rather more beneficial deity concerned with the welfare of the dead, but in Japan he took the form established in China as a judge, and indeed appears with his assistants in Chinese civil-service dress (no. 19). Rescue from the cycle of death and rebirth was through the intervention of the Bodhisattvas, and particularly through Jizō who walks in the six worlds intent upon the salvation of all sentient beings.

Shugendō

Shugendō, the Mountain Religion, was, put at its simplest, an adaptation of the esoteric Shingon and Tendai sects into a Spartan form of asceticism associated with the Shintō gods resident in certain mountains. The sect became associated with the military and included swordsmiths, since their work was concerned with harnessing the most violent forces of nature in the manufacture of their blades, among its most ardent followers. Shugendō might be considered a branch of military studies aligned towards Shintō, as opposed to those traditions which developed under the teachings of Zen. Adepts of Shugendō sometimes claimed special powers like understanding the speech of birds and animals, and the ability of the spiritual body to levitate, whereas the great attainment of Zen was to nullify such preoccupations with the illusory world.

Among images of Shugendō made especially during the Kamakura period were those of the ferocious Buddhist-cum-Shintō deity Zao Gongen (Gongen is a technical term for the appearance in Buddhist form of a Shintō deity) and the mysterious hermit who is credited with being the founder of the religion, En No Gyōja, with his two attendant sprites (no. 25). En No Gyōja's portraits are, like those of Shōtoku Taishi, imaginary, since no original version survives of the eighth-century hermit. But the obvious dominance of the human being over the two demonic sprites who always accompany him is indicative of the confidence in the human spirit which is evident in all Kamakura period portraits.

Zenkōji triad

The Zenkōji-type triad of Amida Nyorai with a Bodhisattva standing either side is named after the Asuka period group in the Zenkōji Temple in

Nagano Prefecture. The triad is said to have been brought to Japan from Korea as a present from the King of Kudara in the sixth century (p. 22), and thrown into a moat at Naniwa (near present-day Osaka) during a political struggle over the intoduction of Buddhism into Japan. The episode is recorded in the *Nihon Shoki*, in which the height of the main figure is given as 1 *shaku* and 5 *sun* (about 45 cm). According to legend a certain Honda Zenkō recovered the images and took them with him to Nagano, installing them in a small chapel which later became the Zenkōji Temple. The figure of Amida stands with the right hand raised and open-palmed, and the left hand pointing downwards with the index and second fingers touching. Many versions of this triad were made during the period, owing to the spread of the Amida faith and out of respect for the origins of Buddhism in Japan.

Seiryōji Shaka

The physical restoration in general of the Nara temples and the revival of the veneration of Shaka Nyorai, particularly in the Risshū sect by priests like Kakusei, Ninshō and Eison, resulted in the manufacture of many images of the historical Buddha. The form which was considered the most authoritative was that of a figure brought back from China in AD 987 by the monk Chonen, which was kept in the Seiryoji Temple. According to an unlikely tradition this image is a copy of an original made in India by King Udayana of Kausambi during the lifetime of Shaka and later taken to China. The legend tells how the King had a sandalwood sculpture of Shaka made to take the place of the Buddha while he was away in heaven preaching to his mother. Upon the Buddha's return the image rose to greet him and was entrusted with the responsibility of spreading Buddhism throughout the ages. Versions of the figure have been considered a kind of manifestation of Shaka since early times in Japan. Several close copies, even using the same kind of wood to give a similar surface and choosing the blocks to give a similar direction to the grain, were made for Risshū sect temples like the Saidaiji, Tōshōdaiji, Shōmyōji (no. 18) and Gokurakuji. The style of garments found on the Buddhas of Gandhara in India, whose origins have been suggested to be Graeco-Roman, is evident in this stylised figure.

CATALOGUE

鎌倉時代の彫刻

1 Kongō Rikishi (Vajrapāṇi)

Wood
Early 13th century
H. (Agyō) 282.0 cm; (Ungyō) 267.2 cm
Nakayamadera Temple, Fukui Prefecture; Important
   Cultural Properties

Kongō Rikishi, also known as Ni-Ō (Two
Kings), are placed as guardians at the gates of
Buddhist temples. Ferocious figures with
vigorous and muscular naked upper bodies,
the guardian with open mouth is known as
Agyō and that with closed mouth Ungyō.
These examples stand at the main gate of the
Nakayamadera Temple in Fukui Province.
Agyō is turned to the right from the waist, with
arms extended and elbows wide apart. In his
right hand he once held a *kongōshō* (a variety
of *vajra*), but the weapon does not survive.
Ungyō stands with his upper body twisted to
the left at the waist, in the opposite direction.
His left hand is stretched down behind and to
the rear, and his right hand makes a fist which
he flourishes in front of his head, the
contradictions producing a startling sense of
tension. The torsos are broad, deep and
muscular. The angry expressions, in figures of
such imposing size, must have indeed
succeeded in creating a feeling of awe in the
believers of the period.

Ungyō (also illustrated on page 35)

Many Kongō Rikishi figures of the Kamakura period are, like these, energetic and vigorous. These examples are typical in that respect and retain a power which was lost in later stylisation. They can confidently be attributed to the early Kamakura period (early thirteenth century), and are among the few to survive from that era.

Both statues are made from Japanese nutmeg, with inlaid crystal eyes. The basic construction is, for Agyō, a head and body composed of three blocks – one for the front, and two pieces left and right for the back. The arms and legs are made from separate pieces. Ungyō is composed of four pieces joined at the centre and sides of the body. The figures were once covered with crude pigments replaced at a later period, but they were removed during recent conservation work to reveal the original appearance of the carvings before they were painted.

Agyō (also illustrated on front cover)

2 Tamon Ten (Vaiśravaṇa)

Wood with pigments and gold leaf
1188–9
Kōkei
H. 197.2 cm
Kōfuk ‿ji Temple, Nara; National Treasure

One of the Shitennō (Four Guardian Kings) who guard the four directions in Buddhism, Tamon Ten guards the North. In many cases the figure is worshipped alone and is known as Bishamon Ten.

This Tamon Ten is one of the four Shitennō who guard the principal deity of the Nanendō hall of the Kōfukuji Temple in Nara, the Fukū Kenzaku Kannon. All four figures are dynamic and rich in variation. Tamon Ten holds in his right hand a *geki* (halberd), and in his left he holds aloft a *hōtō* (treasure tower), which he looks up at. As with the other three guardians the style of the dress is similar to that of the Nara period Shitennō figures of the eighth century. The frame of the body is sturdy, and the depiction of the sinews in the violently angry face and the complexity of the folds in the garment demonstrate vividly the tendency towards dynamic movement in the sculpture of the Kamakura period.

The original figures in the Nanendō were burnt by fire in 1180, and the present principal deity and four guardians were replaced in 1188–9. The temple records tell us that the figures were made by Kōkei and his studio. Kōkei is said to have been Unkei's father and to have been the foundation upon which the Kei school built its position in the mainstream of Buddhist sculptural history throughout the Kamakura period. The four guardians and the main image have always been thought to have been restored by Kōkei in the early Kamakura period. A recent study, however, suggests that the four guardians do not belong in the Nanendō at all, and furthermore that they may be of a later date.

The sculpture is of cypress wood, formed of two pieces joined down the centre, and with the arms and part of the forward leg made separately. The eyes are also carved, with projecting pupils.

3 Bosatsu (Bodhisattva)

Wood
Late 12th century
Unkei or his school
H. 224.7 cm
Manganji Temple, Kanagawa Prefecture; Important
  Cultural Property

This Bodhisattva does not have the
distinguishing attributes usually found on the
heads of standard figures of Kannon, but since
it was always paired with an image of the
Bodhisattva Jizō, it was probably made as a
Kannon attending an Amida Nyorai.

The proportions of this figure, the ample
treatment of the flesh and the fluid lines of the
garment are very similar to those of a figure of
Kannon which is one of the Amida triad in the
Jōrakuji Temple in Kanagawa Prefecture. This
figure is known to have been made in 1189 by
the representative sculptor of the Kamakura
period, Unkei, at the behest of Wada
Yoshimori, a powerful figure in the Kamakura
Bakufu. Other common points in the
construction and style indicate a high
probability that it too was made either by
Unkei or by his studio.

A recent theory proposes that this
Bodhisattva was commissioned from Unkei by
Sahara Jūrō in supplication for the success of
his vendetta against the Heike. Sahara Jūrō
was the father-in-law of Wada Yoshimori, who
built the Jōrakuji Temple and most likely also
commissioned Unkei. Unkei is known also to
have made Buddhist images for the temple
built by his wife Masako's father, Hōjō
Tokimasa. The movement and vigour of
Unkei's sculpture were very much in the taste
of the warriors of Kamakura. After this time
Unkei and the Kei school which he led became
active as the most powerful group of *busshi*,
and Unkei's own reputation grew. As a result
works said to be by Unkei are found scattered
over Japan, although most are later
attributions and few can be proved to be by the
hand of the master.

4 Taishaku Ten (Śakra Derānam Indra)

Wood with pigments and gold leaf
1201
Attributed to Unkei
H. 104.9 cm
Takisanji Temple, Aichi Prefecture; Important Cultural
Property

Taishaku Ten was a military god in ancient
Indian legend. Bon Ten was a god of Creation,
and together they were assimilated into
Buddhism as guardian divinities and placed
either side of Nyorai or Bodhisattvas.

This Taishaku Ten is a Mikkyō figure,
having three eyes, and in his right hand the
single-pronged *vajra*. He was made as the right-
hand attendant of a life-size standing Kannon,
which holds a lotus flower in front of his breast.
The left-hand attendant is a Bon Ten of about
the same size, but with four faces, each having
three eyes, and with four arms. The triad is
believed to have been copied from the principal
deities of the Ninjuden hall of the Imperial
Palace from the Heian period. According to the
history of the temple, the image was made in
1201 by the priest Kanden, a cousin of
Yoritomo, the founder of the Bakufu, in order
to obtain the salvation of Yoritomo himself. In
the central figure, which was made the same
height as the Shogun, were placed some of his
hair and teeth.

The sculptors are said to have been the
father and son Unkei and Tankei, but the
naturalism and powerful and generous
treatment of the flesh are reminiscent of the
Kanagawa Prefecture Jōrakuji Temple figures
made in 1189, which are characteristic works
of Unkei's early period. These pieces are
important sources for the study of Unkei's early
style, together with the Hachi Dai Dōji in the
Kongōbuji Temple on Mount Kōya made in
1197 (no. 5). The pigmentation is much later
than the pieces and presumably replaced the
original decoration.

5 Kongara Dōji

Wood with pigments and gold leaf
1197
Unkei
H. 95.6 cm
Kongōbuji Temple, Wakayama Prefecture (Custodial Body:
    Kōyasan Bunkazai Hozonkai); National Treasure

Kongara Dōji is one of the Hachi Dai Dōji (Eight Great Youths) who attend the figure of Fudō Myō-Ō, the principal deity of the Fudō hall of the Kongōbuji Temple. As the 'right-hand man' of Fudō, Kongara Dōji is said to save believers in the deity. Groups of all eight *dōji* together are rare, and Fudō Myō-Ō is more usually attended by just two, Kongara and Seitaka (no. 22).

According to the temple records the Fudō hall was made under the patronage of Hachijōjoin Akiko Naishinnō in the eighth year of Kenkyū (1197). The image of the principal deity Fudō Myō-Ō was made by the priest Gyōshō, and the Hachi Dai Dōji were made by Unkei. Of the eight, two figures are fourteenth-century replacements, but the six which remain were all made by the same hand. They are very similar to the two *dōji* in the Ganjōjuin Temple of Shizuoka Prefecture which were made by Unkei in 1186, and it is probable that these also were made by him. Furthermore, X-Ray examination reveals moon-shaped tablets inside the figures similar to those found inside the Jōrakuji Temple figures, confirming the probability that this series was made by Unkei.

Both this image and the companion Seitaka Dōji are beautifully painted, with vividly depicted elastic flesh and somewhat cherubic expressions. The figure is made from cypress wood, carved in two pieces joined down the centre. The paint and applied cut gold leaf are of the period. The piece is remarkable for its fine condition.

6 Mi Shin and Inu Shin

Wood with pigments and gold leaf
Early 13th century
Kei school
H. (Mi Shin) 69.2 cm; (Inu Shin) 75.0 cm
Tokyo National Museum; Important Cultural Properties

The Twelve Heavenly Generals were made as
attendants to a figure of Yakushi Nyorai,
whose true believers they protect. The Generals
coincide with the twelve creatures of the
zodiac, which represent a repeating cycle of
years, months, hours and points of the
compass, and some of them have models of
these animals on their heads. They are kept in
the Tokyo National Museum, the Seikadō
Bunko and other places, but they are said to
have once belonged to the Jōruriji Temple on
the outskirts of Nara.

The snake divinity, Mi Shin, with a snake on
his head, is twisted at the waist with his upper
body inclined, menacing an enemy at his feet
with angry eyes and a ferocious shout. The dog
divinity, Inu Shin, from whose hair rises a

Inu Shin

dog's head, holds in his right hand an axe half-hidden behind him and follows the movements of a distant enemy shading his eyes with his left hand. Both figures have elongated trunks, with the lower bodies in stable postures. The arrangement of the upper bodies and arms imparts a sense of movement to their poses. The vivid expressions and the softness of the bodies and clothing are simply but effectively modelled. A similar style can be seen on some of the figures of the Twelve Heavenly Generals in the Tō Kondō of the Kōfukuji Temple in Nara, which were made in 1207. These two figures are thought to have been made by a sculptor of the Kei school also working around that time. The gorgeous colouring and patterns of cut gold leaf are among the finest examples of Nara work.

Mi Shin

7 Amida Nyorai (Amitābha) and attendants

Lacquered wood
Late 12th century
Jikei
H. (Amida) 90.1 cm; (attendants) 106.0 cm, 106.7 cm
Kuwabara Ku, Shizuoka Prefecture

This triad is now kept in the Yakushi Dō Temple hall in the mountains of Kuwabara district, but the figures were originally in the Shinkōji Temple.

The central figure is a life-size Amida, and the two smaller figures are thought to be the Bodhisattvas Kannon (Avalokiteśvara) and Seishi (Mahāsthāmaprāpta). The central figure of Amida has the index and second fingers of both hands crossed in the *raigōin* gesture (one of the attitudes with which Amida descends from Paradise to meet the newly dead). Figures of Amida with this gesture were made in large number from the late Heian period (twelfth century). The Bodhisattva on the right has lost one lower arm, but the two attendant figures looking towards the centre can be seen to have been made as a pair, each facing the central images, from the position of the arms, the turn of the waist, and the bend of the knees.

Inside both figures at the neck portion the name Jikei is inscribed. Jikei was a representative sculptor of the early Kamakura period, and is thought to have been one of the studio of followers of Unkei. In the Shūzenji Temple, not far from Kuwabara, is a figure of Dainichi Nyorai which is recorded as having been made by him in 1210. The Kuwabara Ku Amida triad is thought on stylistic grounds to have been made a little before this Shūzenji figure of Dainichi, and it also has stylistic affinities with the Amida triad in the Jōrakuji Temple made by Unkei in 1189. This triad is therefore a very important surviving example of the early development of the Kei school of Buddhist sculpture in the early part of the Kamakura period.

All three figures are made of cypress wood, carved from one piece, split at the neck and sides of the body and hollowed inside. The eyes are crystal inserts. The bodies were originally covered with gold leaf, but this has fallen off, revealing the black lacquer base layer.

8 Zenmyō Shin

Wood with pigments and gold leaf
1229
Tankei
H. 31.4 cm
Kōzanji Temple, Kyoto; Important Cultural Property

Zenmyō was the daughter of a Chinese aristocrat of the T'ang dynasty who fell deeply in love with Gishō, a priest from the Korean kingdom of Silla, when he was studying in China. When Gishō returned to his native land Zenmyō ran after his ship and cast herself into the sea, changing into a dragon and guarding the ship on its voyage. Gishō founded the esoteric Kegon sect in Silla, and Zenmyō became deified as its guardian.

Myōe Shōnin (1173–1232) of the Kōnzanji Temple had a strong devotion to Zenmyō, and she is accordingly given an important role in the *Kegon Shū Soshi Eden*, which he is said to have compiled. This figure of Zenmyō Shin was commissioned in 1229, when Gyōkan Hōin had it installed as the guardian deity of the Kōzanji Temple. At the same time a figure of Byakkō Shin (originating from a Himalayan deity) was made to form a splendid pair with her.

The deity wears a Chinese T'ang dynasty robe and stands on a rock carrying a small box in her hands. The image possibly represents Zenmyō at the instant of having resolved to jump into the sea. The determined and elevated countenance illustrates the high spiritual status attained by the guardian deity, having transcended the fires of love and passion which racked her body and soul.

According to a much later Edo period source the maker was the master sculptor Unkei's first son, Tankei. The firm expression of the face, the precise sculpting and fine proportions are also found on other work by him. Since the figure has been kept in a *zushi* (portable shrine) behind closed doors the colour has not faded and remains much as it was originally. The cut gold leaf is likewise in its original state, and the box the deity carries is also old, if not the original.

9 Kichijō Ten (Mahāśri)

Wood with pigment and applied gold leaf
1231
Renkei
H. 110.2 cm
Fukkōonji Temple, Yamanashi Prefecture; Important
  Cultural Property

Kichijō Ten originated as the Brahmanic goddess Laksmi, who, since becoming assimilated into Buddhism, has been venerated as the goddess who presides over fortune. Images of Kichijō Ten survive from the Nara period (eighth century). She often appears in a pair with Bishamon Ten, her husband. This example is dressed in Chinese style, as Kichijō Ten normally is, carries in her left hand a *hōju*, and is seated, a rather unusual posture for this deity.

In the Fukkōonji Temple the image is attended left and right by two small figures of Jikoku Ten and Tamon Ten, a rare combination. More unusually still, this figure is heavy in face and figure, and is larger than life-size. Images of Kichijō Ten are generally presented as beautiful and graceful women.

The sculpture is made from two pieces of cypress wood joined along the sides of the body, with arms and legs composed of separate pieces. The eyes are inserted pieces of crystal, and the surface is painted, although much of the pigment has disappeared. The garment is partially decorated with patterns in cut gold leaf. The exact date of manufacture, 1231, and the name of the sculptor are known from an inscription running from the throat to the abdomen inside the figure. The triad comprising this figure and its two attendants was originally made for the Oonoji Temples, which once stood on the site of the present Fukkōonji Temple and was commissioned by government officials in the district. The dais, like the figure, is repaired, but its basic form remains unchanged.

Little is known about the sculptor Renkei, but he is recorded as one of the Kei school of *busshi* who were active in the period, especially in and around Kyoto and Nara.

Also illustrated on page 2

10   Attendants to Jikoku Ten (Dhrtarāstra) and Zōchō Ten (Virūdhaka)

Wood with pigments
1267
Kōen
H. (Jikoku Ten) 31.9 cm; (Zōchō Ten) 32.1 cm
Tokyo National Museum; Important Cultural Properties

The two figures are attendants to two of the Shitennō, the Four Heavenly Guardians of Buddhism who guard the four directions – Jikoku Ten, who guards the East, and Zōchō Ten, who guards the South. There are also attendants for the other two guardian kings, which are not included in this exhibition. The figures originally stood in the Eikyūji Temple in Nara.

Inscriptions on the rock bases of the figures give the names of the guardians, the date of

Attendant to Zōchō Ten

manufacture, 1267, and the name of the sculptor, Kōen. Each figure held a long *hoko*. Their dynamic postures and facial expressions, hair-styles, variations in dress and symmetry immediately show that they are from an interactive group. The exaggeration of the features gives them a humorous air. The dramatic postures and extravagant treatment of the garments are also light-hearted. These small figures demonstrate the individuality of the sculptor Kōen in his mature years.

Attendant to Jikoku Ten

11 The Bodhisattva Monju (Mañjuśrī) and attendants

Wood with pigments
1273
Kōen
H. (Monju) 46.1 cm; (attendants) 46.1 cm, 69.4 cm,
66.5 cm, 70.8 cm
Tokyo National Museum; Important Cultural Properties

This group shows the Bodhisattva Monju and attendants crossing the sea on their way to Godaisan (Wutai shan) in China, where the Bodhisattva was believed to reside. The central figure of Monju rides on a lotus throne on the back of a *shishi* (see no. 34), carrying in his left hand a lotus flower and in his right a sword. The nimbus is pierced and carved with scrolling plants and angelic beings (*apsarases*) to left and right. The youth who leads the procession is Zenzai Dōji (see also no. 13) whose meeting with Monju is described in the *Kegon sūtra*. The figure holding the reins of the *shishi* is understood to be the fervent believer in Buddhism, Uden-Ō. The priestly figure with staff and jewel is Budahari Sanzō, a traveller to Godaisan. The elderly man known as Saishō Rōjin is thought to be the Bodhisattva Monju himself in the form of a Chinese *sennin* (Chinese Daoist immortal) appearing to Budahari.

From an inscription inside the head of the *shishi*, and from documents found inside the figure of Monju, now preserved in the Daitōkyū Kinen Bunko and elsewhere, it is known that the group was made in 1273 and that it was once the principal object of devotion in the Kangakuin hall of the Kōfukuji Temple in Nara. In its sculptural treatment and sense of naturalism it is typical work of the sculptor Kōen, who succeeded Tankei in the main Kei school.

12 Shukongō Shin (Vajrapāṇi) and Jinja Taishō (Shensha Dajiang)

Wood with pigments
Decade before 1203
An-amidabutsu (Kaikei)
H. (Shukongō Shin) 87.0 cm; (Jinja Taishō) 84.5 cm
Kongōin Temple, Kyoto; Important Cultural Properties

A military deity holding a *vajra* in his hand, Shukongō Shin is the origin of the Kongō Rikishi who guard the gates of temples (see no. 1). Jinja Taishō takes the form of a half-naked demon deity, holding a snake, who is said to have appeared to Genjō Sanzō, the Chinese monk of the T'ang dynasty, in order to aid the traveller in his trials in the desert when he was on his way to India after his conversion to Buddhism. He is paired with Shukongō Shin, both of them having the ferocious aspect which intimidates the enemies of Buddhism.

These two figures preserved in the Kongōin have the *gō* (alternative name) of Kaikei, An-amidabutsu, inscribed on the retaining pegs under their feet and are thought to have been made by him some time in the ten years before 1203. In that period Kaikei was, together with Unkei and other *busshi* of the powerful Kei school, working on major sculptures like the two flanking figures for the Great Birushana,

Shukongō Shin

Jinja Taishō

the Shitennō and the Ni-Ō at the Nandaimon (south gate), all in the Tōdaiji Temple, as part of Chōgen's scheme for the restoration of the Daibutsuden there. At this time Kaikei, as a member of the Nembutsu sect, was given the name An-amidabutsu.

This Shukongō Shin is based on an eighth-century clay figure kept in the Hokedō in the Tōdaiji Temple, but the Jinja Taishō is based on late Heian period esoteric Buddhist paintings. Even so Kaikei's strong tendency to seek naturalistic effects is evident in the deeply curved hips and the vigorous set to muscle and sinew in these powerful figures.

Chōgen recorded in his *Sazen Shū* ('A Record of Pious Acts') that he placed images of Shukongō Shin and Jinja Taishō in the great esoteric Buddhist temple complex on Mount Kōya, and it is possible that this pair were those two figures. If so, they must have travelled back to Kyoto at a later date.

13 Zenzai Dōji (Sudhana)

Wood with pigments
1203
An-amidabutsu (Kaikei)
H. 134.7 cm
Monjuin Temple, Nara; Important Cultural Property

Zenzai, according to the *Kegon sūtra*, is the Dōji of Salvation. He appears in the Buddhist legends of India as the son of a rich family, who, in following the teaching of the Bodhisattva Monju, visited fifty-five holy men: finally, hearing the teaching of the Bodhisattva Fugen, he asked to be converted to Amida Jōdo Buddhism.

In paintings Zenzai Dōji is often depicted as the hero of stories of the 'Way of Salvation', but in sculpture he is shown as an attendant of the Bodhisattva Monju. This figure is representative of a type commonly found as one of a group of four attendants to Monju, standing with his hands clasped together and looking back towards the Bodhisattva who rides on a lion.

Inside the head of Monju, the principal deity of the group to which this figure belongs, is inscribed the date, 1203, and a record that the sculpture is the work of An-amidabutsu. This name was used in his early years by Kaikei, one of the most representative sculptors of the early Kamakura period (late twelfth to early thirteenth centuries). The exquisite turn of the head and gaze and the flowing treatment of the garment bring a vivid sense of actuality to the piece. The chisel cuts are deft and strong, a characteristic of Kamakura period sculpture.

The figure is made from cypress wood in the *yosegi zukuri* style with eyes of inset crystal. Part of the painted surface was peeled away and the colours are slightly faded, but on the whole the original appearance is well preserved.

14 Jizō Bosatsu (the Bodhisattva Ksitigarbha)

Wood with pigments and gilt-bronze fittings
Between 1203 and 1210
Kaikei
H. 89.8 cm
Tōdaiji Temple, Nara; Important Cultural Property

Jizō is the merciful Bodhisattva who inhabits Hell and the other of the six worlds of illusion wherein there is no Buddha, during the 570 million years between the death of Shaka and the coming of Miroku, the Buddha to come. He has been venerated in Japan since the late Heian period (tenth century) and is usually shown in the guise of a shaven-headed priest carrying a *hōju* in his left hand and a *shakujō* in his right.

This figure stands in the Kōkeidō hall of the Tōdaiji Temple. A small inscription on the pegs which project from under the feet to fix the sculpture in its base gives the name of Kaikei, who was with Unkei the most important sculptor of the early Kamakura period, together with his Buddhist title, Hokkyō. Since it is known that Kaikei was appointed to the rank of Hokkyō during the interval between the third year of Kennin (1203) and the fourth year of Jōgen (1210), the date of this piece

alone among Kaikei's work is known with some fair accuracy.

The *kyōshoku* (breast ornaments) and *wansen* (bracelet-like ornaments) are of gilt-bronze. This kind of ornamentation is characteristic of Kaikei's work, but the piece is far from stereotyped. The facial expression is particularly youthful, and the piece is a good example of Kaikei's maturity.

The figure is made of cypress wood, the head and trunk portion split along the sides and hollowed out before finishing. The eyes are not of inserted crystal but are sculpted in the wood. The surface is finely painted, with cut gold-foil patterns on the garment.

The lotus pedestal is believed to date from the Kamakura period, but the holes in it do not match the pegs which project from beneath the feet of the statue, so it probably came from another sculpture. The *shakujō*, usually carried by Jizō, and nimbus are missing.

15 Mokkenren (Maudgalyāyana) and Subodai (Subhūti)

Wood with pigments and gold leaf
c. 1220
Kaikei
H. (Mokkenren) 97.2 cm; (Subodai) 98.6 cm
Daihōonji Temple, Kyoto; Important Cultural Properties

These are two of the Jū Dai Deshi (Ten Great Disciples) attendant on the Shaka Nyorai, the main deity of the Daihōonji Temple. Shaka is the historical Buddha, and the Ten were outstanding among his disciples. They are Daikashō (Mahākāśyapa), Furuna (Pūrṇa), Ubari (Upāli), Sharihotsu (Sāriputra), Mokkenren (Maudgalyāyana), Ananda (Ānanda), Anaritsu (Aniruddha), Kasennen (Kātyāyana), Ragora (Rāhula) and Subodai (Subhūti). They are all represented together as a group in the Daihōonji Temple. Mokkenren is said to be the foremost among them and to have had superhuman powers. He is celebrated for having born the suffering of Hell when he travelled there in order to save his mother. Subodai is the one who best understood the nature of Kū ('Nothingness') as the essence of enlightenment.

There is no fixed iconography of the Ten Disciples, but in the Daihōonji version Mokkenren is depicted as an old man pointing to the ground with his finger, and Subodai is shown with mature features and holding a *nyoi*

Mokkenren
(also illustrated on page 2)

(Buddhist sceptre). Treated variously as youths, mature and aged men, the Ten Great Disciples are all carved with realistic features, and although each possesses strong individuality, the harmony of their unity as a group is remarkable.

On the pegs under the feet of Mokkenren which hold the figure in its pedestal, and inside the sculpture of Ubari in the same group, is inscribed the name of Kaikei, the most representative sculptor of the early Kamakura period (late twelfth to early thirteenth centuries). In addition *sutra* material deposited inside the figure of Ananda bears the date 1220 (the second year of the Kenkyū era). It is therefore assumed that the group was made around that time by Kaikei and his school, and is typical of his style in portraiture in his last years.

The figures are of cypress wood, each of a block split down the sides of the head and body and hollowed out. The eyes are inset crystal. The surface is pigmented and decorated with patterns in cut gold leaf.

Subodai

16 Amida Nyorai (Amitābha)

Wood with lacquer and gold leaf
1235
Gyōkai
H. 98.6 cm
Amidaji Temple, Shiga Prefecture; Important Cultural
  Property

Amida Nyorai was very widely venerated as
the ruler of Gokuraku Jōdo, the Pure Land
Paradise. Many figures of this Buddha have
been made since the middle Heian period
(tenth century) when Jōdo became widely
transmitted through Japan. This figure has the
first and second fingers of each hand crossed,
with the right hand raised and the left hand
lowered, the conventional standing figure with
the so-called *raigōin* hand gestures, welcoming
the believer into Amida's paradise. The type
has been popular since the late Heian period
(twelfth century), but this particular very
beautiful form was originally perfected by
Kaikei, one of the major sculptors of the early
Kamakura period. The Amida figures of Kaikei,
who is known also by the Buddhist name
An-ami, have deeply influenced subsequent
Amida sculptures in both style and form.

From documents found inside the statue, and
from an inscription on the pegs on the underside
of the feet which retain the figure in its
pedestal, it is known that it was made by Gyōkai
in 1235 (the second year of the Bunrayaku
era). Regarded as the greatest among Kaikei's
pupils, Gyōkai is especially known for having
sculpted the Shaka Nyorai figure which is the
principal deity of the group of figures in the
Daihōonji Temple in Kyoto made by Kaikei's
studio. This version has the balanced
proportions characteristic of Amida images in
Kaikei's style. However, the facial expression is
somewhat sterner, and the strongly carved
features and thickset appearance of the body
show an individual creativity which separates
the work from that of Gyōkai's master, Kaikei.

The figure is of cypress wood, split at the
neck and down the sides and hollowed out.
The eyes are of inserted crystal. The surface is
rather worn but is decorated with gold leaf on
lacquer. The nimbus and lotus throne are later
additions.

17 Nyoirin Kannon (Cintāmaṇicakra)

Wood with lacquer and gold leaf
c. 1256
School of Jōkei II
H. 99.3 cm
Tōgenji Temple, Kyoto; Important Cultural Property

Nyoirin Kannon is one of the aspects of the merciful Bodhisattva Kannon (Avalokiteśvara) who has many different forms and virtues. The deity has been worshipped in Japan since the early Heian period (ninth century) and appears in both painting and sculpture. According to the early iconographic descriptions the Nyoirin Kannon can have either two or four arms, but there are many versions like this one with six.

Inside the carefully hollowed-out interior of the sculpture there was deposited a copper *sūtra* holder containing a *sūtra* with an inscription stating that its copying out was commissioned in 1256 by the priest Enkū (1227–84) for the Hachijōin of the Dai Jion Ritsuji Temple. From this the approximate date of manufacture and the first home of the figure can be deduced.

The high hair-style of the figure and the floral decoration on the crown, the waves in the hanging tresses, the long fingernails, and the rippling folds along the hem of the skirt all suggest the Chinese Song dynasty style, possibly reflecting the influence of the sponsor Enkū, who had been to China. This tendency is often found on Kamakura period pieces and was especially favoured by Higo Betto Jōkei, who established his school of sculpture in the early thirteenth century. This example is somewhat stylised and belongs to a slightly later period when the manner had hardened.

There is no reason to doubt the information found inside the figure, and it can be supposed to have been made by a sculptor who was probably a pupil of, and working in, the generation after Jōkei. The Hachijōin used to lie close to and to the east of the Tōkaidō line Kyoto station and owned a large tract of land. The Dai Jionji Temple was built within the Hachijōin grounds, but neither the date of its destruction nor when this figure was transferred to the Tōgenji Temple is known.

18 Shaka Nyorai (Śākyamuni)

Wood
1308
Inpo
H. 160.6 cm
Shōmyōji Temple, Kanagawa Prefecture; Important
    Cultural Property

The principal deity of the Seiryōji Temple in Kyoto is a Shaka Nyorai brought from China in the tenth century by the priest Chōnen. It was made by sculptors of the Song dynasty, modelled on a sandalwood figure which legend held to have been made in India during the lifetime of Shaka. The Seiryōji Shaka is therefore thought to be imbued with the spirit of three countries. Shaka was especially venerated in the Kamakura period by the priest Eison, who established the Shingon Risshū sect at the Saidaiji Temple. Many sculptures were made based on the image during the period.

From an inscription found inside this figure during conservation work it is known to have been made in 1308. The main sculptor is identified as Inpo, and in addition a number of In school sculptors and devotees of Eison were involved in the project. The head and body, the modelling of which is rather angular, are composed of two pieces hollowed out and joined along the sides, the joint being skilfully concealed. The flesh and robes are depicted in a heavy and rigid manner in common with other works of the In school sculptors. The wood is nutmeg, which is close in texture to the Seiryōji original. The surface is also finished in imitation of the original, with the lines of the garments and patterns applied over the garment with cut gold foil.

19 Gushō Shin and Ankoku Dōji

Wood
First half of 13th century
In school
H. (Gushō Shin) 114.5 cm; (Ankoku Dōji) 110.5 cm
Hōshakuji Temple, Kyoto; Important Cultural Properties

These are two figures from a spectacular group of five, of which the central figure is the King of Hell, Emma-Ō, from Hoshakuji, a temple in the suburbs to the west of Kyoto. The two form a pair and, according to the temple records, they are called Gushō Shin and Ankoku Dōji. Gushō Shin settles on the shoulder of the newly born to remain there throughout the individual's life recording his good and evil acts in order to report them to Emma-Ō when he dies. The figures are thought to have been originally made as Shimei (or Shimyō) and Shiroku, the names by which similar images are known in other temples. Shimei and Shiroku are officials present at court when Emma-Ō judges the crimes of the deceased. Since there are no other known examples of the companion figure, Ankoku Dōji, his exact function is not clear. He wears a high cap and sits with one leg tucked up on his chair, over which is draped the skin of a beast.

Ankoku Dōji

Gushō Shin

Gushō Shin unfurls a scroll; Ankoku Dōji holds a brush in his right hand and in his left a wooden writing tablet. As officials of Hell they both have stern faces, their bodies are sturdy, and the figures are as a whole full of vigour. The treatment of the garments is naturalistic, but unexaggerated, in keeping with the style of the early Kamakura period (first half of thirteenth century).

The figure of Juichimen Kannon (Ekādaśamukha, 'Eleven-headed Kannon'), the main deity of the Hōshakuji Temple, is known to have been made by a sculptor named Inpan in 1233. Inpan was one of the In school of influential sculptors who worked mainly for the imperial court and nobility. These two figures may also be the work of the In school.

The figures are of cypress wood, with the block forming the trunk and head split into four pieces and hollowed out. The arms and legs are carved from separate pieces. The eyes are of inserted crystal. The surfaces were once painted, but the pigment has all disappeared.

20 Shidda Taishi (Prince Siddhārtha)

Wood with pigments and gold leaf
1252
Inchi
H. 54.2 cm
Ninnaji Temple, Kyoto; Important Cultural Property

This figure of a youth wearing his hair coiled up in bundles in front of his ears is shown to be an aspect of Buddha by the spot between the eyebrows. He wears Chinese T'ang style dress and a *tenne* (heavenly garment). According to a document found inside the figure when it was disassembled for conservation work, it represents Shidda Taishi (Siddhārtha) or Shaka (Śākyamuni) before he left home, and it was made in 1252 by the sculptor Inchi. There are no other known extant works, nor is there any further information about Inchi, but from his name he must have been one of the In group of sculptors who were active from the late Heian period and had a studio in Kyoto serving the court and nobility.

The style is confident and expresses the humanism of the period. The figure has great stability from the head to the knees, and the whole treatment of the face and garment is quite restrained. The rich effects of painting on silk seem to have been the model for the flowing shape of the sleeves and the intricately carved folds in the lower garment. The figure has crystal inset eyes, and is pigmented and decorated with cut gold leaf.

21 Aizen Myō-Ō (Rāgarāja)

Wood with pigments and gold leaf
Early 14th century
H. 59.6 cm
Agency for Cultural Affairs, Tokyo; Important Cultural
  Property

Aizen is the Myō-Ō, or King of Light, who represents the authority of Dainichi Nyorai, the principal deity of esoteric Buddhism, who is identified with the Sun God. Sculptures and paintings of Aizen Myō-Ō have been made since the Heian period as the principal tantric image which nullifies the sin and anguish which arise from desire, and overcomes enmity and calamity.

It is not known from where this particular example originated, but painted on the doors of the *zushi* which contain it are the group of deities which form the Aizen Myō-Ō *mandala*, and on the *tengai* (overhead canopy) is painted the Shuji Butsugen *mandala*. It is therefore known that the object must have been connected with the founder of the Shingon Risshū sect in the latter part of the period – the

priest Eison, of the Saidaiji Temple in Nara.

The figure wears a crown surmounted by a *shishi*. The hair is swept upwards. A sheet of crystal is used for the three eyes, and the fangs are revealed in the open mouth. The six hands hold characteristic symbols of esoteric Buddhism, including a bow and arrow. There is a necklace over the bare red torso, and the figure is clad in a robe richly coloured and decorated with gold foil. The deity sits on a lotus throne above a vase from which treasures cascade, and has a circular halo in representation of the Sun.

The form of the image is standard and typical of the early fourteenth century in its childlike proportions and treatment of the flesh. It is remarkable for the excellent condition of its rich colouring.

22 Kongara Dōji and Seitaka Dōji

Wood with pigments and gold leaf
Late 13th-early 14th century
H. (Kongara) 54.9 cm; (Seitaka) 22.9 cm
Jōshōan Temple, Shiga Prefecture; Important Cultural
  Properties

These two *dōji* are attendants upon Fudō Myō-
Ō (Acalanātha), representative of the angry
forms of the Myō-Ō (Kings of Light). Fudō is
accompanied by the Hachi Dai Dōji (Eight
Great Youths), but in many instances there are
only the two *dōji*, Kongara and Seitaka. Triads
of Fudō and the two *dōji* were popular from the
late Heian period onwards.

  The forms of Kongara and Seitaka are not
fixed. These from the Jōshōan have Kongara
standing and holding a lotus flower, with
Seitaka seated on a rock and holding a staff.
The passivity of Kongara contrasts with the
dynamic figure and unearthly facial expression

Kongara D

of Seitaka. Such a contrast between the two is often found on Kamakura period examples.

The figures are made of cypress wood. The block is split along the sides of the body and neck, and hollowed out prior to assembling and finishing. The eyes are inset crystal. Although the pigment has degraded in places, the overall effect remains very beautiful. The garments are partially decorated with cut gold foil. The standing figure is just 50 cm tall, but is exquisitely carved and a fine example of the delicacy achieved in the late Kamakura period. The attributes and plinths are later additions.

Seitaka Dōji
(also illustrated on page 3)

23 Shōtoku Taishi

Wood with pigments and gold leaf
Mid-13th century
H. 152.8 cm
Shōkōji Temple, Ishikawa Prefecture

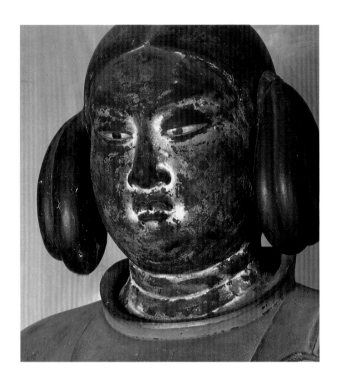

Shōtoku Taishi (574–622) conducted the government of Japan and foreign affairs as Regent on behalf of his aunt, the Empress Suiko, from AD 593 to 622. He established the situation to encourage the growth of Buddhism in Japan, building the Hōryūji Temple in Nara and the Shitennōji Temple in Osaka.

During the Kamakura period the veneration of Shōtoku Taishi as the supposed founder of Japanese Buddhism, an emanation of the historical Buddha himself, flourished, particularly in Nara. Images of him at the ages of two (no. 24), sixteen and thirty-two were made for this cult. This figure represents the sixteen-year-old Shōtoku praying for the recovery from illness of his father, the Emperor Yōmei, with his hair coiled in bunches behind his ears, and holding a long-handled censor.

The broad and deep-bodied statue is carved with the delicate line admired in the princely class. From its style the piece is believed to be a mid-thirteenth-century work by a sculptor working in Nara. The well-preserved pigments are close to those of paintings of the same period, and few pieces of the time have survived in such splendid condition.

24 Shōtoku Taishi

Wood with pigments
Early 14th century
H. 70.0 cm
Daisenji Temple, Osaka

This version of Shōtoku Taishi, known as a Namu Butsu Taishi, shows the two-year-old in the attitude he is said to have adopted at that age, facing East and proclaiming the words 'Namu Butsu' ('I trust in Buddha'). The iconography is traditional, the upper body being naked and the lower body clothed in a red *hakama* (broad pleated divided skirt), and with the hands clasped in prayer. The flesh of the upper body is convincingly childlike, and the face is set in an aspect of precociously acquired wisdom. Many similar figures were made after the thirteenth century, and this relatively early example dates from the early fourteenth century.

The figure is made from cypress wood by the *yosegi zukuri* method. The eyes are of inset crystal, and the surface is painted. A small piece of the hem of the *hakama* is missing from the back of the figure.

25 En No Gyōja and two attendant sprites

Wood
13th century
H. (En No Gyōja) 112.5 cm; (sprites) 47.6 cm, 48.8 cm
Ishibaji Temple, Shiga Prefecture; Important Cultural
   Properties

The religious personage En No Gyōja derives from a real person named En No Ozune who lived an ascetic life around the end of the seventh and beginning of the eighth centuries. He lived on a mountain called Katsuragisan near to the capital and used magical practices. Various legends grew around him, to become embellished in later times; he is credited with being the founder of the Shugendō religion, an esoteric combination of Buddhism and Sangaku, or Mountain Religion. En No Gyōja's portrait is found frequently in temples which have a connection with Shugendō, but there survive no statues of him which predate the thirteenth century.

The figure is a standard version, wearing a cloth cap, with the bearded face of an old man and the legs visible below the hem of the lower garment. In his left hand is a rosary and in the right a staff. He sits on a rock dais, wearing high single-bladed *geta* (wooden sandals). The ascete is shown in a hollowed-out background representing the cave in which he lived. On the left and right are the two followers of the 'hermit' – Zenki, with open mouth and holding a water bottle, and Kōki, with closed mouth and carrying an axe. The aged body of a hermit ravaged by many years of ascetic practice is skilfully depicted. In the characteristic demonic expressions of his followers more than a trace of humour can be detected.

The three figures are made of cypress in the *yosegi zukuri* method, with eyes carved in the wood. The surfaces were once painted, but that has long since fallen away, and the wooden figures now bear the patina of age. The stands and movable attributes of the three figures, the face of Zenki, and the right forearm and back of the head and trunk of Kōki are all later additions or repairs.

26 Basū Sennin

Wood with pigments
1308
Eiken
H. 77.0 cm
Jōrakuji Temple, Shiga Prefecture; Important Cultural
  Property

This is one of the Nijūhachi Bushu, a group of twenty-eight figures arranged to the left and right of a seated figure of Senju Kannon (Thousand-armed Kannon), who is the principal deity of the Hondō hall in the Jōrakuji Temple. The figures are followers of the Senjū Kannon, mostly Heavenly Beings (Ten), but Basū, holding a *sūtra* scroll in his left hand and supporting himself with a stick in his right, is an elderly human figure.

The name Eiken, presumed to be the sculptor, is inscribed on the inside of the head against the face, with the date of manufacture, 1308 (third year of the Tokuji era). Little is known of the *busshi* Eiken, but the piece is a fine characteristic work of the late Kamakura period. A similar piece is included among the well-known twenty-eight figures in the Rengeōin of Kyoto (the Hall of the 1,000 Buddhas), made in the middle of the thirteenth century, the period of the finest flowering of Kamakura sculpture. Even though this version from the Jōrakuji Temple has notable differences from the Rengeōin pieces, they share the dramatic naturalism which is the main characteristic of Kamakura sculpture.

The figure is made from cypress wood in *yosegi zukuri* style, and has inset crystal eyes. The surface is painted, though much of the pigment has flaked off or degraded. The scroll and stick which the figure holds and the dais are later additions.

Also illustrated on page 38

27 Zendō Daishi (Shangdao)

Wood with pigments
Second half of 13th century
Kyoto sculptor
H. 77.4 cm
Zendōin Temple, Kyoto

Zendō (613–81) was a Chinese Jōdo priest of
the early T'ang dynasty who studied under
Dōshaku and compiled the *Tariki Jōdo Kyōgi*,
the theory of salvation through *tariki* ('other
strength' – that of Buddha), as opposed to *jiriki*
('self-strength'). He became revered as the third
of the five patriarchs of the Jōdo sect, and his
teaching had a profound effect on it in Japan.
Hōnen established his own Jōdo movement
having 'entered the Way' of the Nembutsu and
been inspired by the four scrolls of Zendō's
great work, *Kan Mu Ryō Ju Kyō Sho*, a
commentary on the Mu Ryō Ju *sūtra* which
describes the forty-eight vows of Amida.

Although no portraits of the priest survive in
China, according to records there was one in
the Zendō Eidō ('Hall of the Zendō Image') in
the capital of Changan at the end of the eighth
century. There are no surviving images of
Zendō in Japan which predate the Kamakura
period, but many were made from the
thirteenth century when the Jōdo sect

expanded. Most versions have the hands
clasped and the face inclined with the mouth
slightly open chanting the Nembutsu, as in this
example. This rather unusual sculpture is said
to be based on a figure of Zendō in the *Hōnen
Denkie* picture scroll, which illustrates the story
that Zendō visited Hōnen in a dream and
inspired him to found his version of the Pure
Land worship.

There are no extant life-size versions of the
portrait – all other pieces are the same size as
this example. The fitting together of the carved
pieces is fine, and the sculpture has been
finished with care and delicacy. The movement
of the muscles around the mouth intoning the
Nembutsu is modelled with great refinement,
and the pigments are correspondingly delicate.
The piece dates from the second half of the
thirteenth century and was probably made by
a sculptor working in Kyoto itself.

Also illustrated on page 21

28 Minamoto Yoritomo

Wood
2nd half of 13th century
H. 70.6 cm
Tokyo National Museum; Important Cultural Property

This portrait of Minamoto Yoritomo, the first
Shogun of the Bakufu military government at
Kamakura, is known to have originally
belonged to the Shirahata shrine of the
Tsuruoka Hachiman shrine complex at
Kamakura. He is depicted in ceremonial
hunting dress, wearing an *eboshi* (court cap)
and carrying a *shaku* (sceptre). Other similar
portraits of warriors include, in the Meigetsuin
at Kamakura, the figure of Uesugi Shigefusa
(dates unknown but mid-thirteenth century), a
court official who joined the Bakufu at
Kamakura, and from around the same time,
kept in the Kenchōji Temple at Kamakura, a
portrait of Hōjō Tokiyori (1227–63) who held
the highest appointment of Regent in the
Bakufu.

All these portraits are similar in technique of
manufacture, and are thought to have been
made around the same time, but only the
sculpture of Uesugi Shigefusa is finely executed
both in facial detail and in the treatment of the
clothing, and may be a portrait from life.
However, the portrait of Yoritomo, made half
a century after his death, might be said to
express the greatness of the man through the
swirling lines and billowing of the garment.
The eyes are of crystal, and the original
pigmentation has long since disappeared.

Also illustrated on page 13 and back cover

29 Shunjō Shōnin (the priest Chōgen)

Wood with pigments
Early 13th century
H. 87.7 cm
Amidaji Temple, Yamaguchi Prefecture; Important
  Cultural Property

Chōgen (1121–1206) first studied Mikkyō, later becoming a believer in Amida Nyorai, and assuming for himself the name Nanamida Butsu. He was half-way through his life when the Tōdaiji Temple was rebuilt after the conflagration of the fourth year of the Jishō era (1180). He became fund-raiser for the work on the Tōdaiji Temple, and also built temples in the provinces in order to obtain the safety and salvation of the people involved in the reconstruction of the temple.

Portraits of Chōgen also exist in the Daibutsuji Temple of Mie Prefecture, in the Jōdoji Temple of Hyōgo Prefecture and in the Shujōdō of the Tōdaiji Temple itself. They were all made in the Kamakura period, but according to one study this Amidaji Temple version was made in the first year of the Kennin era (1201), before the death of Chōgen, while the others are all memorial pieces made after his death.

Compared with the Tōdaiji portrait, which is known to have been made in 1206 shortly after Chōgen's death at the age of eighty-six, this image has a youthful appearance. It is thought to represent the priest when he was engaged in the rebuilding of the Tōdaiji, having been granted by the court the right to cut wood from the forests in Suō Province, where he obtained large timbers for building the new Daibutsuden (Great Buddha Hall).

It is unusual to find a piece carved from a single block of wood at a time when the *yosegi zukuri* technique had become widespread. Perhaps it reflects the abundance of large trees available at that time in Suō.

30 Tairako Shigetsune

Wood
After 1224
H. 87.6 cm
Genkyūji Temple, Yamaguchi Prefecture

Tairako Shigetsune was a warrior in the
service of Minamoto Yoritomo, who
established the Bakufu government at
Kamakura. In 1197 he achieved a military
success and was rewarded with the lordship of
the province in which the Genkyūji Temple
stands, a position which he held for twenty-
eight years until his death. During the first year
of the Shōji era (1199) he built the temple as
a memorial where prayers could be offered for
the salvation of the deceased Yoritomo, and at
the same time for the fortunes in war of his
successors in the Tairako clan.

   Shigetsune died in 1224 and was buried in
this temple; the figure was probably made
within just a short time of his death. His head
is shaved and he wears a *kesa*, showing that he
had entered the priesthood. The position of his
hands indicates that he is holding a rosary. The
wrinkled texture of the flesh of the face clearly
shows that the portrait was made during
Shigetsune's last days, but the sound muscles
and bone structure, and the robust hands,
suggest the strength of the Kamakura warrior
class.

   There are a number of portraits of priests of
the period, but few of warriors having entered
the priesthood. The body is made from four
blocks, and the two legs together of one block.
The hollow inside the body bears the marks of
crude chiselling. The maker of this rare and
important piece is thought to have been a
provincial sculptor.

31 Ryōgen

Wood with pigments
Shortly after 1251
H. 76.0 cm
Zenpukuji Temple, Kanagawa Prefecture

This portrait of a seated priest with his two hands clasped before his chest was once identified as Shinran Shōnin, founder of the Jōdo Shinshū sect, but comparison with documented figures of Shinran has shown that not to be the case. There is now firm evidence that this portrait is of Ryōgen, the founder of the Zenpukuji Temple.

Ryōgen was born in the fourth year of the Kenkyū era, 1193, after the death of his father, Jūrō, in the turmoil of a military action. It is said that his father was the elder of the two Soga brothers who avenged the death of their father in a fight at the Fuji Susono Makigari festival. The Revenge of the Soga Brothers was later to be celebrated as one of the Three Great Acts of Revenge in Japanese history, and is today widely known as the subject of song and Kabuki drama.

Ryōgen achieved renown in military action during the Wada disturbance of 1213, and in reward was given the district of Hiratsuka in Sagami Province by the Shogun Minamoto Sanetomo. He was converted by Shinran of the Jōdo sect when he visited the region, and entered the priesthood later to build the Zenpukuji Temple. He died in March of 1251 at the age of sixty. This portrait is thought to have been made in the normal way as an object of veneration immediately after his death, but it might have been made while he was still alive, perhaps at the time of the consecration of the temple.

The full figure, wearing a *kesa* (priest's surplice) and seated with hands clasped, is sculpted in an expressive style. It is possible to sense from this piece the spiritual stature of Ryōgen, who forsook the world to enter the priesthood, in the figure's bountiful smile as he chants the Nembutsu.

32 Donshō Risshi

Wood with pigments
c. 1259
H. 80.5 cm
Kaikōji Temple, Kyoto

Donshō is the *gō* (alternative name) of Jōgō
(1187–1259). Born in Kyoto in 1187, he went
to China at the age of twenty-seven to study
Ritsugaku (teaching of the Risshū sect) for
fourteen years, returning to Japan in 1228. He
built the Kaikōji Temple near the Kyōōgokokuji
Temple as a *kairitsu dōjō* (hall of religious
discipline). In 1233 he returned to China to
bring back to Japan Sanskrit *sūtras* and
Buddhist images. He then built a temple at
Daizaifu in Kyūshū and another in Kyoto.
Donshō engrossed himself during his final
years in the recital of the Nembutsu and died
at the age of seventy-three in 1259.

This image shows Donshō intoning the
Nembutsu in his advanced age. It is venerated
as the founding image of the Hondō hall of the
Kaikōji Temple, when it was moved to the
south of the Sennyūji Temple. The peaceful
character of the priest is suggested by the
gentle expression on the finely sculpted
almond-shaped face. The inserted crystal eyes,
in particular, express an air of gentle
benevolence. Details such as the differing shape
of the ears suggest that the sculpture is an
accurate representation of the subject. It might
have been sculpted from life, or it must have
at least been made under the guidance of
someone who was familiar with the Jōdo
devotions of the priest, if, as seems more
probable, it had been made shortly after his
death.

During the Kamakura period the Zen sects
used to make images of their deceased chief
priests, serving them as if they were still alive.
The custom spread to other sects after the
middle Kamakura period, and this is an early
example of that practice.

Also illustrated on page 45

33 Taa Shōnin (the priest Shinkyō)

Wood
Early 14th century
H. 83.3 cm
Shōganji Temple, Yamanashi Prefecture; Important
   Cultural Property

Taa Shōnin, the honorific title for Shinkyō (1237–1319), was a prominent priest of the Jishū faction of the Jōdo sect, founded by Ippen in the middle Kamakura period (mid-thirteenth century). He succeeded Ippen, like him travelling around the country converting people of all classes, especially the peasantry.

This life-sized portrait of Taa Shōnin has been preserved in the Jishū Jiin, which he founded within the Shōganji Temple complex. The figure sits wearing a simple *kesa*, with his hands clasped. It has much in common with portraits of Jishū sect priests made in large numbers from the end of the Kamakura period (beginning of the fourteenth century). However, the figure is austere with a simply carved body and sparse decoration on the robes. The lifelike features are carved even with the distortions of mortal illness, and the portrait is therefore thought to have been made not long after the death of Shinkyō in 1319. A wooden model of a lotus found inside the neck is probably an object closely associated with Shinkyō during his lifetime.

The figure is made of cypress wood, the head composed of one major block with the face carved from a separate piece. The whole is hollowed out, and the eyes are inlaid crystal. The body is composed of four pieces joined along the centre and sides, and is also hollowed. The lower body components are inserted into it. The surface was originally painted, but most of the pigment has flaked off, and the figure now appears black.

Also illustrated on page 43

34   Koma Inu

Wood with pigments
13th century
H. (Agyō) 98.5 cm; (Ungyō) 95.4 cm
Shirayamahime Jinja Shrine, Ishikawa Prefecture;
Important Cultural Properties

Koma Inu were, since the Heian period, pairs
of lion-like guardian beasts placed before the
seat of the deities of Shintō shrines. They are
also known as *shishi*, usually translated as
'lion-dogs'. The use of lion-like guardians was
imported from China via Korea and ultimately
from further west still. They normally sit with
straight forelegs, and like the Ni-Ō figures
which guard the gates of temples (see no. 1),
that on the right, Agyō, has its mouth open,
and that on the left, Ungyō, has its mouth
closed. In many cases the beast on the left has
a single horn in the centre of its head. The
origin of the term Koma Inu ('dog of Koma' –

Ungyō

a country of ancient Korea) is thought to have derived from the two *shishi* who enter the stage of the Komagaku form of the courtly Bugaku drama before the main performers.

This large pair have been preserved in the Shirayamahime Jinja Shrine, where they originally guarded the path which led to the holy place sacred to the Sangaku cult on the Shirayama Mountain. Some characteristics of the sculpture of the period can be seen in the heavy proportions of the heads and set of the forelegs, the movement of the sinews stretched along their backs and the rigorous, deeply carved faces.

Agyō

35 Tateyama Shin

Bronze
1230
H. 49.0 cm
Toyama Prefecture; Important Cultural Property

This figure is known from the inscription carved on the body and front of the pedestal to have been cast in 1230 in a temple on Mount Tateyama, one of the sacred mountains of Japan, and was venerated as the god of the mountain. It is recorded that six copies of the *Nyohō sūtra* were once placed inside the statue, but they are no longer with it.

The deity wears a crown, a long pleated garment and shoes. The style of the sculpture is very similar to the Ten figures of Buddhism, but the angry expression and the stance with both elbows raised are characteristics peculiar to, and frequently found on, figures of the Shintō gods of Japan. The posture which does not quite correspond with the movement of the long body, the restrained treatment of the flesh, and the long controlled lines which represent the garment are all characteristic of the simpler style used for images of Shintō deities.

The figure and the pedestal are cast in bronze, with the arms formed of separate castings joined at the shoulders. The hands are also made separately from the wrists down. All the parts are thin-walled hollow castings made using cores. The eyes and lines of the garment have been tooled over with chisels. There is no evidence of gold plating over the bronze. Both the object which was once held in the two hands, and the nimbus, are missing.

Also illustrated on page 1

36 Sōgyō Hachiman Shin (Hachiman in priest form)

Wood with pigments
Early 14th century
H. 51.5 cm
Shōmyōji Temple, Kanagawa Prefecture

The Shintō god Hachiman is said to have originated as the God of Production of the immigrant Korean clan, the Hata, who practised the 'burned fields' method of agriculture in north Kyūshū. In the Nara period (eighth century) the god Hachiman was invoked in Nara in order to enlist his aid for the timely completion of the Tōdaiji Temple. From around that time the deity became associated with Buddhism and was known as the Bodhisattva Hachiman. Images of him which show Buddhist influence were made, and those depicting the god as a priest are known as 'Sōgyō Hachiman Shin' (priest-form Hachiman Shin). The earliest known example is the figure in the Hachiman Shin triad in the Kyōōgokokuji Temple of Kyoto, made at the direction of the priest Kūkai (Kōbō Daishi) in the ninth century. In general he is shown in a triad together with two female deities. However, from the Kamakura period onward, beginning with the example by Kaikei in the Tōdaiji Temple, many single images are known.

This piece from the Shōmyōji Temple is one such example. The god is shown wearing a *kesa* and with a *shakujō* in his right hand. Although there is no supporting evidence for the date of manufacture, the style suggests that it is from the early fourteenth century. The face is reminiscent of a Chinese *rakan* (*arhat*), showing the influence of Chinese paintings of these disciples of the Buddha from the Song and Yuan dynasties. During the Kamakura period the ancient emperor Ōjin, whose mother was the Jingū Kōgō who is said to have subjugated the three nations of Korea in the fourth century, became recognised as a manifestation of the deity. Hachiman Shin acquired the special devotion of the Kamakura samurai as the god of the bow and arrow, and many early provincial pieces exist showing him in that role.

37 Daikoku Ten (Mahākāla)

Wood
Early 14th century
H. 56.3 cm
Nara National Museum

Daikoku Ten originated as the Indian god Mahākāla, who was introduced into Buddhism as a guardian deity. In Japan he is sometimes depicted as a martial deity with an angry expression, but he is also found in temple kitchens and other rooms as a god of food, drink and fortune. Popular figures of Daikoku Ten from the Kamakura period onwards have him wearing a *zukin* (cloth cap), carrying a large sack over his left shoulder, a mallet in his right hand, and standing on rice bales. Since that time he has been popularly worshipped as a lucky deity, one of the Seven Gods of Good Fortune.

This figure of Daikoku Ten has an amiable expression and wears the cloth cap which typifies him. Running figures like this are extremely rare in Buddhist sculpture. It might have been made by special request in the hope that good fortune should be brought more quickly to the sponsor by the running deity. The piece can be securely dated to the late Kamakura period (fourteenth century) by the extremely naturalistic treatment of both body and dress.

The sculpture is made of cypress wood, the body and trunk being formed from a single block which has been split at the body, face and neck, and the interior then hollowed out. The arms and legs are formed from separate pieces. The eyes are inset crystal. The plinth is a later replacement.

38 Amida Nyorai (Amitābha) and two attendant Bodhisattvas

Bronze
1300
H. (Amida) 48.3 cm; (attendants) 34.7 cm, 34.9 cm
Seikōji Temple, Chiba Prefecture; Important Art Objects

This triad is thought to be patterned on the model group in the Zenkōji Temple, Nagano Prefecture. It is said that the figures were brought from the Korean kingdom of Kudara when Buddhism was introduced into Japan in the sixth century. Versions of the original, like this triad, were made when devotion to Amida was promulgated throughout Japan by the activities of the Jōdo sect from the early Kamakura period onwards. Many similar cast-bronze pieces were produced during the late Kamakura period, particularly in eastern Japan. Several versions of the triad are stylised and simplistic, and betray the hand of the metal founder rather than that of the *busshi*. This is one such example.

The shape and height of the figures correspond with the oldest examples prior to the seventh century both in Korea and Japan; but the large nimbus, which would originally have covered the backs of the figures, and the bases are missing. On the back of the central Amida and on one of the attendants are inscribed the date, 1300 (the second year of the Shōan era), and the names of more than thirty male and female divines who had some connection with the commissioning of the triad.

GLOSSARY

Agyō The open-mouthed figure of a pair of Ni-Ō guardians or *shishi*, situated on the left of a temple or Shintō shrine.

Bakufu The 'Camp Curtain Government', formed by the samurai, the hereditary military class. The first Bakufu was formed at Kamakura in 1185 by Minamoto Yoritomo, following his victory over the Taira clan.

bessho A country house or provincial affiliated temple.

Bosatsu (Bodhisattva) A being who has attained the level of enlightenment necessary to become a Nyorai but who has postponed the ultimate state in order to promote the salvation of mankind.

busshi A specialist sculptor of Buddhist images.

byakugō A whorl of hair in the centre of the forehead, an attribute of a Nyorai. On images it is often represented by a piece of inlaid crystal.

chinzō A standard form of Zen priest's portrait in which the subject is seated in a high-backed Chinese-style chair.

dogū Low-fired stylised pottery human images, probably connected with fertility rites, made predominantly from the Middle Jōmon (c. 3,000–4,000 BC) era. They have been unearthed near hearths in domestic dwelling excavations.

dōji Literally 'youth'. Attendants of certain deities.

eboshi Tall cap worn by aristocrats and high-ranking warriors.

geki Pole-arm carried by guardian deities. See also *hoko*.

geta Wooden sandals with one or, more usually, two horizontal wooden blades raising the flat soles above the ground.

gō An alternative name adopted by a mature artist or craftsman.

gyokugan Crystal eyes set from behind the face of a wooden image.

hakama Man's divided skirt, or wide pleated trousers.

haniwa Low-fired red pottery models of humans, animals, buildings, boats and various artefacts made during the Kofun ('Great Tombs') era (c. second to seventh centuries AD) and set upright in the ground in the vicinity of tombs.

Hīnayāna (Minor Vehicle) An early form of organised Buddhism with a priesthood which expounded the teachings of Buddha as a means of salvation for only a certain category of people.

hoko Halberd carried by guardian deities. See also *geki*.

hōju The jewel which grants desires, an attribute of Nyoirin Kannon, Jizō Bosatsu and other deities.

hōtō 'Treasure tower'. Attribute of the guardian Tamon Ten or Bishamon Ten and other deities in the form of a pagoda-like tower.

ichiboku zukuri Method of wood sculpture prevalent before the late Heian period for Buddhist images, whereby the figure is sculpted from a single block, which might be partially hollowed and have separate pieces for the limbs.

The defect of the method was the incidence of splitting owing to changes in the moisture content of the wood and the limitation on the size of images which could be made.

Jōdo (Sukhāvatī) The Pure Land, a paradise ruled over by Amida Nyorai, where the meritorious will find salvation.

jōhaku The upper body garment of a Bosatsu, Myō-Ō or Ten, worn diagonally from the left shoulder to the right of the trunk.

jōroku butsu A standing Buddhist image about 16 ft (4.9 m) in height. 1 *jō* = 10 *shaku* and 6 (*roku*) *shaku* (about 1 ft, or 30.3 cm) was believed to have been the actual height of the historic Buddha.

kami The gods of Shintō.

kanshitsu Literally 'dry lacquer'. Method of manufacture of Buddhist images prevalent during the Nara period rather like papier mâché, using hemp soaked in lacquer to form outer layers over a rough model of wood or clay, which might be removed leaving a thin-walled, hollow figure.

kesa A priest's surplice, which fives diagonally over one shoulder.

kokubunji A monastery or nunnery decreed in AD 741 by the Emperor Shōmu (r. 724–49) to be built in every province.

Kongōkai The 'Diamond World', or ultimately real world according to esoteric Buddhism.

kongōsho (vajra) An implement of esoteric Buddhism deriving from an Indian weapon. Usually of gilt-bronze, it is held by the centre, both ends having blunt points, either one, three, five or nine. The *kongōsho* is the attribute of certain guardian deities and Bodhisattvas and is used by priests in ritual.

Kū Literally 'Nothingness'. The nullification of the illusory world, hence enlightenment.

kyōshoku The breast ornaments of the necklace of a Bodhisattva.

Mahāyāna (Greater Vehicle) The form of Buddhism developed in China and prevalent throughout the Far East, according to which there is a pantheon of deities who assist living beings towards salvation.

mandara (Japanese), mandala (Sanskrit) Schematic representations of Nyorai and Bosatsu representing the impermanent (Taizōkai) and ultimately real (Kongōkai) worlds according to esoteric Buddhism.

mantra (Sanskrit), mantara (Japanese) Spoken magical charms in esoteric Buddhism.

Mappō The last of the three periods of the Buddhist law signifying its destruction before the coming of the next Buddha, Miroku, and thought to have commenced during the eleventh century.

Mikkyō Esoteric Buddhism in which the wisdom of the main Buddha of the sect, Dainichi Nyorai, can be received through the practice of elaborate ritual. See also Shingon.

mo The skirt of a Bosatsu.

Myō-Ō   The 'Kings of Light', manifestations of aspects of Dainichi Nyorai according to Mikkyō.

nehan (Japanese), *pari nirvana* (Sanskrit)   The physical death and ascension into Paradise of the historic Buddha.

nyoi   A form of sceptre with a turned-over trefoil tip.

Nyorai   A Buddha – a wholly enlightened being. The historical Buddha, Shaka Nyorai, lived *c.* 500 BC. There have been numerous Nyorai in aeons past and Nyorai yet to come. Through a succession of rebirths all beings might become Nyorai in time, although the next expected is the Bodhisattva Miroku, whose ultimate enlightenment will occur in 5,670,000,000 years from now.

rakan, arakan (Japanese), *arhat* (Sanskrit)   A Buddhist saint, or enlightened human being for whom there is no rebirth, such as the disciples of the historic Buddha. They are frequently depicted in groups of sixteen or 500.

satori   The attainment of spiritual enlightenment.

sennin   A Chinese Daoist hermit immortal.

shaku   Narrow fan-shaped sceptre of aristocratic office.

shakujō   A priest's staff which has a finial of loose iron rings which jangle, thus warning minor creatures of the priest's approach.

Shingon   Esoteric Buddhist sect brought from China and established in Japan in AD 806 by Kūkai, or Kōbō Daishi (773–835).

Shintō   'The Way of the Gods'. The indigenous naturalistic religion of Japan before the introduction of Buddhism.

shishi   Lion-like beasts placed in pairs at the gates of temples and before the residence of the deity in Shintō shrines. Like the Ni-Ō guardians, that on the right (Agyō) has an open mouth, and that on the left (Ungyō) has a closed mouth. Ungyō sometimes has a single horn on his head. The sculptures are often known as Koma Inu ('dogs of Koma' – a country of ancient Korea).

Shitennō   The 'Four Heavenly Guardians', or 'Four Guardian Kings', military deities who guard the four directions.

Shugendō   Sect of ascetic hermits associated with esoteric Buddhism and the Shintō deities residing in certain mountains.

sōhei   Warrior monks. The Buddhist temples of Japan during the Heian period became very powerful and kept garrisons of armed monks to protect their land and other interests.

sūtra (Sanskrit)   A discourse of the Buddha.

Taizōkai   The 'Matrix World', or the illusory world according to esoteric Buddhism.

tatchū   A complex of small-scale living quarters for Zen priests separate from the main buildings of their temple.

Ten   The guardian deities of Buddhism originating from Hinduism.

Tendai   Sect based on the Lotus *sūtra* and containing elements of Shingon introduced into Japan by Saichō, or Dengyō Daishi (767–822).

tengai   A decorative circular canopy which hangs over the head of a Buddha, originating from a sunshade.

tenne   A long scarf-like garment worn over both shoulders of Bodhisattvas and guardians.

Ungyō   The closed-mouthed figure of a pair of Ni-Ō guardians or *shishi*, situated on the right of a temple or Shintō shrine.

vajra (Sanskrit)   See *kongōsho*.

wansen   The bracelet-like arm bands of a Bodhisattva.

yosegi zukuri   Method of manufacturing images developed during the late Heian period and prevalent during the Kamakura period, whereby a number of separate blocks are hollowed out and joined together. This reduced the danger of the sculpture splitting owing to stresses in the wood and provided for large-scale sculptures.

zukin   A simple everyday cloth cap as worn by the deity Daikoku Ten.

zushi   A shrine with doors for documents or images. Small versions were carried on the person.

BIBLIOGRAPHY

SIR CHARLES ELIOT, *Japanese Buddhism*, Routledge & Kegan
   Paul Ltd, London, and Barnes & Noble Ltd, New York,
   1969

Japanese Sculpture of the Kamakura Period, exhibition
   catalogue, Tokyo National Museum, 1975

HISASHI MORI, *Shozō Chōkoku*, Nippon Bijutsu Series No.
   10, Shibundō, Tokyo, 1967

HISASHI MORI, *Sculpture of the Kamakura Period*, vol. 11 in
   'The Heibonsha Survey of Japanese Art', Heibonsha,
   Tokyo, 1974

KYOTARO NISHIKAWA, *Ichiboku Zukuri To Yosegi Zukuri*,
   Nippon Bijutsu Series No. 202, Shibundō, Tokyo, 1982

SHINJI NISHIKAWA, *Kamakura Chōkoku*, Nippon Bijutsu
   Series No. 40, Shibundō, Tokyo, 1969

YOSHIYASU TANAKA, *Kamakura Chihō No Butsuzō*, Nippon
   Bijutsu Series No. 222, Shibundō, Tokyo, 1983

SABUROSUKE TANOBE, *Unkei To Kaikei*, Nippon Bijutsu Series
   No. 78, Shibundō, Tokyo, 1972

WILLIAM WATSON, *Sculpture of Japan*, The Studio Ltd,
   London, 1959